From six continents, seven seas, and several archipelagoes,

From points of land moved to wind and water

Out of where they used to be to where they are,

The people of the earth marched and travelled

To gather on a great plain.

CARL SANDBURG, *The People Yes*

America Fever

the story of American immigration

Barbara Kaye Greenleaf

FOUR WINDS PRESS/NEW YORK

FOR REPRINT PERMISSION, GRATEFUL ACKNOWLEDGMENT IS MADE TO:
Harcourt, Brace & World, Inc. for "The People Yes" by
Carl Sandburg, copyright, 1937, by Harcourt,
Brace & World, Inc.; copyright, 1964, by Carl Sandburg.

First printing, 1970
Second printing, 1971

Published by Four Winds Press
A Division of Scholastic Magazines, Inc., New York, N.Y.

Printed in the United States of America
Library of Congress Catalogue Card Number: 72-105335

For Jonathan

CONTENTS

Nova Britannia.
OFFERING MOST
Excellent fruites by Planting in
Virginia.

Exciting all such as be well affected
to further the same.

London
Printed for Samvel Macham, and are to besold at
his Shop in Pauls Church-yard, at the
Signe of the Bul-head.
1 6 0 9.

Europeans were often lured to America by leaflets describing the golden
opportunities to be found in the New World. This is one of the earliest
examples of such advertising, dated 1609. NEW YORK PUBLIC LIBRARY

Peopling the Colonies

"WHY LIVE IDLY AND SOFTLY AT home when you may live well and nobly in New England?" John Smith asked his fellow countrymen. But despite Captain Smith's own enthusiasm for America, few Englishmen cared to join him in so exhausting and dangerous an occupation as pioneering. Through bitter experience all colonizers discovered that manpower is the most valuable—and most scarce—element in a new country. Smith recalled that it cost "many a forgotten pound to hire men" for Jamestown, the first permanent British settlement in North America. Governor Peter Stuyvesant complained that New Netherland was "only gradually and slowly peopled by the scrapings of all sorts of nationalities (few excepted), who consequently have the least interest in the welfare and maintenance of the commonwealth."

The labor shortage that plagued European colonizers has

been at the root of all mass migration to America. In the seventeenth century the problem was compounded by the high price of a transatlantic voyage, which was far beyond the means of most Europeans. It remained for profit-minded ship captains to devise the indenture system of signing up men in Europe, shipping them to America and apprenticing them here. The trade in all types of bonded servants grew so brisk that it eventually accounted for one-half to two-thirds of all colonial immigration south of New York.

❧ INDENTURED SERVANTS

Long before the New World was discovered, men apprenticed themselves to masters to learn a trade and receive support. Englishmen did not consider it strange, therefore, when Jamestown's original settlers agreed to work for the Virginia Company—which owned the land—for seven years in exchange for their passage to America and food, clothing and shelter. When the men had finished their term of service they were free to return to England or stay on in the settlement. Those who remained struck out on their own instead of offering themselves as salaried laborers. They asked the Virginia Company to send indentured servants whom they would hire. The Company agreed and the planters were so pleased with the results that in 1619 John Pory wrote from Virginia, "Our principall wealth consisteth in Servants."

Merchants as well as colonizers soon discovered a source of wealth in indentured servants. The ship captain who "bought" an indentured servant in Europe could count on "selling" him for as much as eighty-four dollars in America, a sum far above actual transportation costs. The merchant then applied this amount toward his purchase of colonial products. In fact, he probably exchanged the servant directly for tobacco or some other raw material because colonists had very little cash in circulation. When the merchant returned to Europe, he sold his American goods at a handsome profit.

As the transportation of servants grew into an important item of colonial trade, merchants competed for cargoes. They sent agents throughout Europe to stir up interest in the New World. These agents were generally shady characters who wheedled, tricked and even kidnapped children and adults. The most common offense of "Spirits" or "Newlanders," as Europeans contemptuously referred to them, was misrepresentation. A report from northern Ireland in 1729 stated that ship captains "send agents to markets and fairs . . . to assemble the people together, where they assure them that in America they may get good land without either paying tithes, or taxes, and amuse them with such accounts of these countries as they know will be most agreeable to them." One of the agents' songs was directed to "merry London Girls, that are disposed to travel." The song promised them that they could get rich from the gold and silver mines of Virginia and live on "fare most dainty." Except when a spontaneous desire to leave—often called a "fever"—swept parts of Europe, agents were behind all emigration in colonial times.

Once the "Spirit" convinced a prospective servant that life would look much rosier in the New World, the actual indenturing process was simple. The recruit merely signed a standard contract. As early as 1636 the system had become so common-place that one could easily obtain a printed form with blank spaces for the servant's and master's names. The contract stated that the servant was to work for a set term, usually four years, during which time he would receive room, board and clothing in addition to his passage to America. At the end of his term he was awarded "freedom dues": some combination of money, tools, clothes and land. Skilled workmen sometimes added a clause exempting them from field work. Children's indentures, which usually bound them until the age of twenty-one, specified that they be taught a trade or given an elementary education. Many German indentures often entered into servitude on the condition they be taught to read the Bible in English.

Immediately after he signed the contract, an indenture often found himself imprisoned. Ship captains kept servants on board their vessels, in houses on shore and even in the town jail lest they run away. During the eight- to ten-week voyage to America, servants lived in constant fear of their lives. The ships, hundreds of times lighter than today's ocean-going vessels, were at the mercy of the seas and winds as well as hostile navies and pirates. At best, passengers were seasick for most of the voyage; at worst they became seriously ill due to the unsanitary conditions of shipboard life. As Philadelphia or Newcastle— the main ports of entry for servants—came into view, captains did their best to spruce up their shipments. They had the men wash their faces, cut their hair, straighten their clothes and even don wigs to make them look more respectable. When the boats docked, the servants were assembled on deck so planters could interview them and feel their muscles. The servants were then auctioned off to the highest bidders. So great was the demand that captains disposed of their entire cargoes in a few days. Toward the end of the trade, "soul drivers" bought whole lots of servants and drove them from town to town like cattle, dispersing them along the way.

Since free labor in the colonies was in short supply, somewhat undependable and often three times as expensive as in England, colonists knew they had a bargain in bonded servants. But the term of indenture was short and many masters wanted to be sure they got their money's worth. In the early years they drove their servants so hard that the back-breaking regime combined with crude living conditions caused over 50 per cent of the servants to die. Indentured servants were considered private property. They could not marry without their masters' consent, nor could they engage in trade or vote and those who ran away were severely punished. Although servants had more legal rights than slaves, their everyday life was not very different. In a popular English ballad one victim sang:

> Five years served I, under Master Guy,
>   In the land of Virginny, O,
> Which made me for to know sorrow, grief and woe,
>   When I was weary, weary, weary, weary, O.

As harsh as conditions were for servants in the colonies, America offered the poor man a better opportunity for advancement than Europe. For the hardy and intelligent, the time of servitude was not necessarily wasted. They became seasoned to the colonial climate and ways of living and working. Many of the indentures learned a trade during their apprenticeship. When their service was over they were completely free and there was no stigma attached to them because so many colonists had started out under indenture. Indeed, a few ex-servants rose to positions of importance. As early as 1629 seven former indentures sat in Virginia's governing House of Burgesses and fifteen had seats in the Maryland Assembly of 1637. Charles Thomson, secretary of the Continental Congress, Matthew Thornton, a signer of the Declaration of Independence, and Matthew Lyon, a Congressman, entered the colonies under indenture. But these were not typical servants, for only 20 per cent became landowners, artisans or overseers on plantations. The overwhelming majority either died in servitude, returned to England or occupied humble positions in colonial life.

It was somewhat easier for indentured women to advance themselves. They started out cleaning and serving in manor houses, milking cows or hoeing tobacco alongside men. But in the early years, particularly, they were in great demand as brides. In 1649 one British author advised "that man that's full of Children to keepe his Sonnes in England, and send his Daughters to Virginia, by which means he shall not give but receive portions for all his Children." Immigrants to the British colonies rarely intermarried with native Indians, and white women were highly prized because they were scarce. The importation of women assured a transference of European stock to America. This was not true of the Spanish and Portuguese colonies of Latin America, however, where widespread intermarriage between conquerors and Indians formed a new people.

❧ REDEMPTIONERS

During the seventeenth century, indentured servitude was almost the only way a poor person could get to the colonies or white labor could be supplied to American planters. As the colonies became better established, however, more substantial farmers and tradesmen were tempted to immigrate to the New World. A new system was invented to facilitate their trip, and in the eighteenth century more people traveled to the colonies as redemptioners than as servants.

The redemptioner system developed on the Continent when the Germans and the Swiss began to emigrate in large numbers after 1708. Many of the emigrants traveled to the main ports on the Rhine River, where they had to pay tolls at thirty-six customs houses along the way. When they reached Rotterdam or Amsterdam after a journey of four weeks they found that their depleted resources could not cover the fare to America. But merchants were eager for their business, so they took whatever money the travelers had left, transported them to America and allowed them two weeks after arrival to pay the balance of the fare. The waiting period gave immigrants a chance to contact friends and relatives who might advance them the money to "redeem" themselves. If the necessary amount could not be found, captains sold the passengers into servitude, their length of service being determined roughly by the size of their debt—usually two years. Nearly all Germans who did not pay their own passage came to the colonies as redemptioners. Many Englishmen, too, traveled under redemptionist agreements, although not as many as under indenture.

[*15*]

Once the redemptioner was transferred to an American master he was treated exactly like an indentured servant. But there were certain differences between the two groups. Indentured servants came singly and, indeed, were required to do so by British law after 1682. Redemptioners usually emigrated in families. When they arrived here sometimes only one member was "sold," but often families were broken up and members, including children, were indentured to masters in different colonies. Indentures often signed up for the New World to escape grinding poverty or jail, while redemptioners came here as immigrants seeking a new home and better way of life. Many servants, too, had hopes for themselves in the New World, but they emigrated essentially because merchants wanted to make a profit out of transporting them. Since redemptioners moved with furniture and other equipment and were generally a sounder lot, they succeeded far better in the colonies than most indentured servants.

◄₹ CONVICT LABOR

Most colonists thought poorly of bonded servants. They agreed with the Georgia Trustees who concluded that "many of the Poor who had been useless in England were inclined to be useless likewise in Georgia." Colonists held this opinion, in part, because they failed to distinguish between regular indentures and convict servants.

The breakup of feudalism and the growth of cities had led to an upheaval in British society. Thousands of people without jobs or homes began to wander around the country, sometimes stealing what they needed. Respectable Englishmen became alarmed as crime spread and they made ever-harsher laws in an effort to control the situation. Eventually Britain's "Bloody Code" designated three hundred crimes, mostly against property, punishable by death. A man could be hanged for fishing in a squire's pond or cutting down his trees. To make the law more reasonable, judges spared a convict's life if he would leave the country. Those who agreed to exile were turned over to private merchants, who made a large profit from transporting them—in chains—to Maryland, Virginia and other colonies. The British sent 30,000 convicts here, mostly thieves, as well as hundreds of beggars, wandering children, and Irish and Scottish prisoners of war.

The British considered sending convicts to the colonies a humanitarian act. And from all evidence, the transportees ate better, lived more healthfully and had a better chance for advancement in the New World than in a London prison or slum. But many returning convicts said they would rather be hanged than transported a second time, so great was their suffering in America. Nor did the colonists look upon the influx of thousands of murderers and thieves as "humanitarian." Colonial newspapers were filled with accounts of their lawlessness and men from all walks of life protested the British practice of "dumping" them here. Yet despite complaints against the importation of convicts and colonial laws forbidding it, the British never had to force convicts on the colonies. Tobacco planters from Maryland and Virginia hastened to seaports where they might take advantage of this cheap source of labor. While redemptioners were bonded for two years and indentures for four, convicts were transferred for at least seven years and they generally received no freedom dues. When they had worked off their indentures, most convicts returned to England or moved to other parts of the colonies under assumed names. Fewer than 10 per cent became substantial figures in America.

✒ THE SLAVE TRADE

"Why then will Americans purchase Slaves?" wrote Ben Franklin, a founder of the abolition movement. "Because Slaves may be kept as long as a Man pleases or has Occasion for the Labour; while hired Men are continually leaving their Masters (often in the midst of his Business) and setting up for themselves."

While Negro slavery was the dominant means of production in the West Indies, it was slow to gain acceptance in the thirteen colonies. The first Negroes to arrive in Jamestown, in 1619, were sold as indentured servants. Some of the Negroes who followed in the next three decades were slaves, but most were indentures, and in time Virginia had a considerable number of free blacks. One community of free Negroes owned hundreds of acres and imported both African slaves and British servants. When a worldwide demand for tobacco led the colonists to develop huge plantations, they sought cheap labor in numbers that not even convicts could supply. The planters wanted men who would be forced to work for them for life and whose children would be similarly bound. In short, they wanted slaves. Indians were considered and quickly eliminated because they tended to sicken and die in captivity. A few Europeans were enslaved in the West Indies, but they were protected by strong governments and, in any case, could escape too easily into the general body of free colonists. Negroes seemed ideal because they had no powerful governments interested in protecting their rights and were indelibly marked by their color. Moreover, their supply seemed inexhaustible.

At first colonists justified slavery on religious grounds because Africans were heathens. Any slave who professed Christianity was freed. But then the colonists, who, like other Europeans, believed blacks to be naturally inferior, shifted the basis for slavery to race. In 1664 Maryland declared that any Negro in the colony was a slave for life by virtue of color alone. Three years later Virginia reversed its earlier ruling with a law that stated: "The conferring of baptism doth not alter the condition of the person as to his bondage or freedom." From then on not all Negroes in America were slaves, but all slaves were Negro.

The slave trade started in 1444, when the Portuguese imported Africans to work their fields. Later, Europeans and natives captured African men, women and children on a regular basis in exchange for whiskey, beads, guns—even old sheets. They marched the captives in large caravans to ports on the continent's west coast. There, the captives were examined and only those under thirty-five and in good health were selected for the New World. The chosen ones were branded on the chest with a trading company's mark and herded onto slave ships. One-third of them died on the long march to the coast and another third perished on the infamous "middle passage" to the colonies. This contemporary description bears out the allegation that slave ships were floating torture chambers:

On many of these ships the sense of misery and suffocation was so terrible that in the 'tween-decks—where the height sometimes was only eighteen inches, so that the unfortunate slaves could not turn around, were wedged immovably in fact, and chained to the deck by the neck and legs—that the slaves not infrequently would go mad before dying or suffocating. In their frenzy some killed others in the hope of procuring more room to breathe. Men strangled those next to them and women drove nails into each other's brains.

Despite heavy losses, ship captains often made a 100 per cent profit on their human cargoes. Colonists paid dearly for slaves and prices were constantly going up. In 1754 George Washington paid $260 for a male slave, while ten years later he had to pay twenty-five dollars more for another one. Even in those days, however, easy credit terms were available and some slavers required only a small down payment for their merchandise. Once Negroes were declared servants for life, the importation of slaves rose dramatically. Some 200,000 were brought into the colonies in the eighteenth century. Although slaves were sent to every region, 90 per cent were bought for use in the South.

While still in Africa, many black people poisoned themselves or jumped into shark-infested waters rather than be taken to the New World in bondage. Many of those who survived the "middle passage" found life so intolerable in the colonies that they ran away, disobeyed all orders and plotted to kill their masters and burn down the plantations. To control the slaves, Virginia enacted a stern "black code" in the seventeenth century which was widely copied. For major offenses, such as robbery, a slave was to receive sixty lashes and have his ears cut off. For minor offenses, such as insolence or associating with free Negroes,

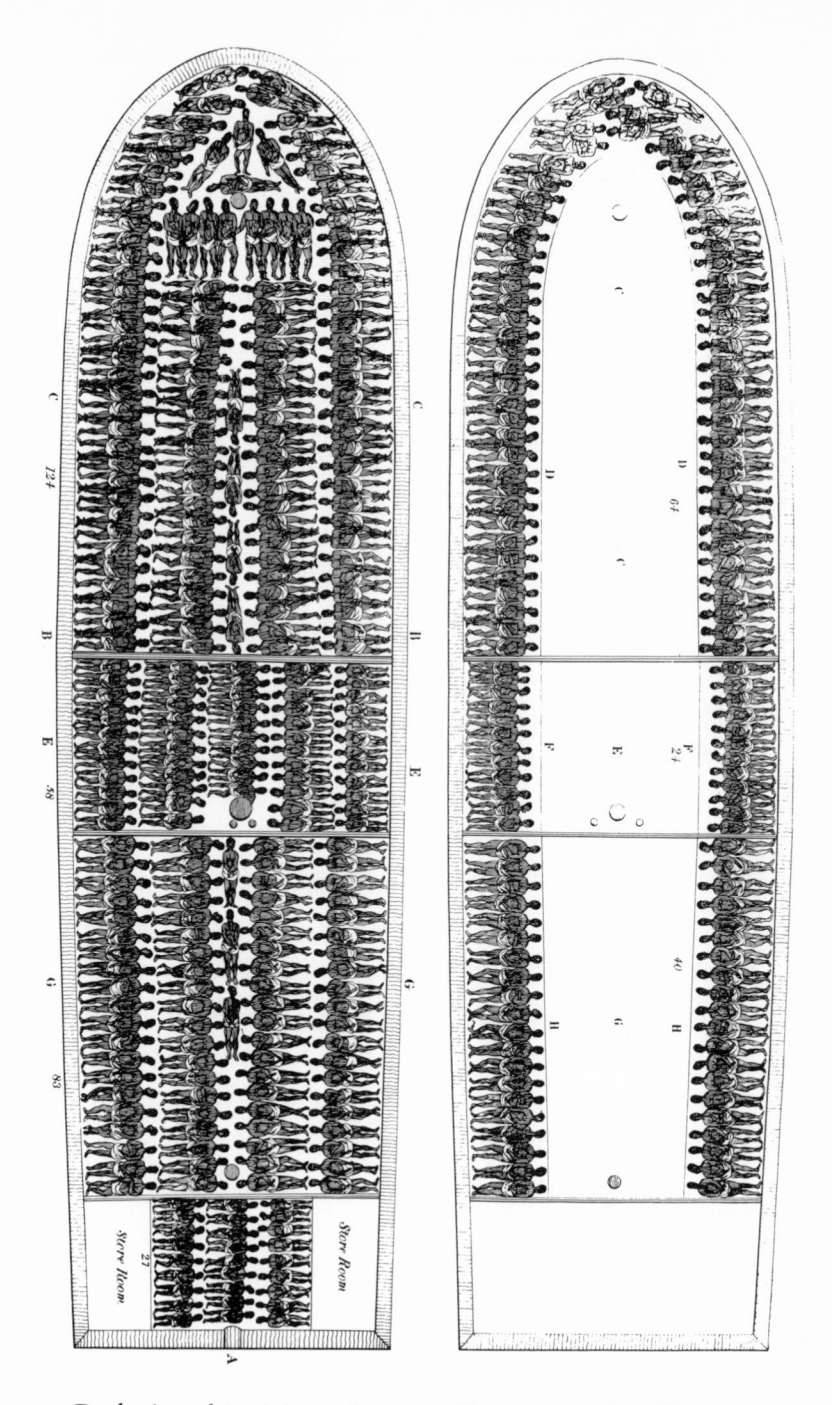

Deck plan of an eighteenth-century British slave ship. The intense crowding illustrated here caused some slaves to suffocate and drove others insane. NEW YORK PUBLIC LIBRARY

he was to be whipped, maimed or branded. Black codes allowed the slave no court of appeal, and white public opinion, even that of non-slaveholders, sided with the master in every case. Although colonists devised these laws to "break" the most intractable slaves, Negro protest continued as long as slavery itself.

๙ THE PURITANS

In 1620, one year after the first Negroes sailed into Jamestown Harbor, one hundred and two Pilgrims stepped off the *Mayflower* at Plymouth on Massachusetts Bay. The Pilgrim Fathers were the advance guard of thousands of Puritans who fled England. The Puritans wanted to simplify services in the Church of England and reform a corrupt British society. In the early seventeenth century they faced increasing harassment for their beliefs, including expulsion from universities and church pulpits. Obtaining a charter in 1628 from the Massachusetts Bay Company, the Puritans decided to quit England and join their fellow dissenters, the Pilgrims, in the New World. The Puritan exodus of the 1630's is called the "great migration." Contemporaries noted the "incredible numbers" who sold their lands in a "great giddiness" to depart. Whole communities led by their ministers rose up, and before the "America fever" had subsided, twenty thousand Puritans were established in communities around the site of present-day Boston.

The Puritans sought out the American wilderness so they could establish a truly holy colony free of European decadence.

Like other frontiersmen, early Puritan settlers were
constantly on guard against hostile Indians. As
this painting shows, they even had to carry guns to
and from Church. Courtesy of the NEW YORK
HISTORICAL SOCIETY, NEW YORK CITY

They thought of themselves as "a city upon a hill with the eyes of all people upon them." In their efforts to make a success of their experiment in Christian living, they demanded strict conformity from all inhabitants. The Puritans earned a reputation for heartless discipline, and the "Puritan tradition" in American life came to mean censuring the behavior of others. The Puritans influenced Americans for many generations in remote parts of the country both because they moved away from New England and because they trained the majority of early ministers, who studied at their colleges. When the newly ordained preachers took up pulpits in villages and cities across America, it was Puritan ethics they expounded. Through countless Sunday sermons, Americans came to believe that wasting time was a sin and material success was a sign of virtue.

We usually think of the Puritans sitting in church hour after hour, but in reality they lived like other frontiersmen, for Boston was on the frontier of its day. The Puritans spent their time clearing land, sowing and harvesting crops and building barns. They established one important industry in drying cod and another in distilling West Indian rum. For relaxation Puritans gave dinner parties, went to picnics and held other lively get-togethers. As frontiersmen, self-defense was uppermost in their minds and many of their puzzling laws stemmed more from practical considerations than religious convictions. For example, one of the famous Massachusetts Blue Laws prohibited young boys from loitering in the woods. This was not so much because "an hour's idleness is worse than an hour's drunkenness" but because the youths could have been attacked by Indians hiding among the trees.

Most of the Puritans who came in the "great migration" were middle-class farmers, tradesmen and craftsmen and all were British. They brought few indentured servants with them, nor did they care to have this class follow after. According to a letter dated 1723, New Englanders obliged "all Masters of ships to carry them [servants] back again upon their owne charge, or else they must not trade in this country." The magistrates of Massachusetts Bay examined each newcomer with great thoroughness. They returned some newcomers to England "as persons unmeete to inhabit here" and the governor could order a month's probationary period for anyone he thought unfit "to sit down among us without some trial of them." As the tide of immigration swelled, the Puritans became even more restrictive, forbidding any individual or community from boarding a stranger more than three weeks except by special order. In the Puritan settlement of New Haven, townsmen not only refused to grant land to undesirables, but they sometimes "whipped and sent out of the plantation" newcomers who did not meet their standards.

The handful of non-Englishmen who lived in New England were absorbed by the Puritans. Many of the Scots were bachelors and they were prized as husbands for Puritan daughters. Germans and Frenchmen anglicized their names and Catholic Irishmen gave up their religion, becoming indistinguishable from the rest of the population. By the time of the Revolution, New England's exclusive immigration policies made it the smallest and most homogeneous of all colonial areas. Finding a cold welcome and little work in New England's family-size businesses and farms and being unable to compete with slave labor in the

[25]

The Quakers were one of the many groups who
came to America to escape religious persecution.
Here, a contemporary artist depicts a British
Quaker being tortured for his beliefs.
NEW YORK PUBLIC LIBRARY

South, most immigrants turned their sights toward the Middle
Colonies. Pennsylvania was the goal of many.

✐ THE QUAKERS

When Quakers reached Massachusetts Bay, the Puritans condemned them as "a cursed set of hereticks lately risen up in the
world." The colony's General Court banished the Quakers several
times and, when they returned, it ordered harsher punishments
including cutting off their ears. In 1658 Virginia called for a
"general persecution" of Quakers. To save his co-religionists from
savage treatment like this in Europe and America, William Penn
founded a colony with land given him by the British Crown in
1681. While the Puritans established Massachusetts Bay to pro-

mote their own beliefs, Penn intended Pennsylvania as a haven for people of all religions and ways of life.

William Penn did not leave his colonization plans to chance. He hired agents to spread the word and he himself traveled widely, lecturing about the colony in the British Isles and on the continent of Europe. Penn also wrote *Some Account of the Province of Pennsylvania,* which was translated into German, French and Dutch and circulated throughout Europe. This advertising campaign and the liberal land terms he offered—such as a 200-acre tenant farm at a penny-an-acre rent—interested Europeans in Penn's woodlands. Indeed, Penn had so many applicants that he did not have to adopt the widely used head-right system, whereby settlers received a land bonus for recruiting new colonists.

Quakers from Ireland and Wales were the first to take Penn up on his offer. They were spared the hardships of other pioneers because several hundred Swedes and Finns remaining from the short-lived empire of New Sweden were already settled around Philadelphia. Provided with food and some of the amenities of civilization, these early Quakers made rapid progress in developing the colony. Soon other religious dissenters joined them. Mennonites, Inspirationalists, Schwenckfelders, Moravians and others immigrated in large numbers. Great Britain often assisted these persecuted Europeans in getting to the colonies. Once there, they were free to retain their own beliefs, yet they could become naturalized citizens and enjoy all the rights of British subjects.

Many of Pennsylvania's immigrants—sectarians or not—entered the colony as indentures and redemptioners. Their services were in great demand since the Quakers opposed slave labor and the large Quaker establishments required many hired hands. In the eighteenth century the largest immigrant group, the Scotch-Irish, made Pennsylvania their home. These hardy settlers had lived for many years as pioneers in Ulster, in northern Ireland, and they brought hundreds of practical skills with them when they emigrated. After working for a time in settled areas, many Scotch-Irish set off for the Carolina back country and the Virginia Valley, where they became America's typical backwoodsmen. The second largest immigrant group in the eighteenth century, the Germans, also considered Pennsylvania their promised land. As redemptioners they were impatient to start those productive farms that became the envy of all America.

Despite minor squabbles between immigrant groups, Penn's "holy experiment" was a great success. For the first time people of all nations and religious sects lived under the same government on equal terms—and in peace, if not brotherly love. The attitude of Pennsylvanians was the forerunner of the national policy of toleration that made America famous around the world. An official church had been designated by law in almost every colony and dissent was usually prohibited. But these churches had little influence in the eighteenth century and, with the coming of a variety of sects, religious liberty became a practical necessity. Jews, particularly, benefitted from the tolerant atmosphere. They enjoyed greater religious and political freedom in the colonies than anywhere else in the world, particularly after 1740, when they became eligible for citizenship. Between two thousand and three thousand Jews, mostly Portuguese and Spanish merchants, clustered in seaports such as Newport, Philadelphia, New York and Charleston.

THIS NEW MAN, AN AMERICAN

Although Pennsylvania had a particularly varied population, it was by no means the only cosmopolitan area in North America. New York had a very mixed population due mainly to the popularity of its port on the Hudson. Even as New Amsterdam, part of the Dutch colony of New Netherland, New York City attracted an international assortment of sailors, French planters from the Caribbean and Portuguese Jews fleeing persecution in Brazil. The Dutch had "imported" Scandinavians and Germans to build up and defend the colony and they, too, added to its cosmopolitan flavor. When the British took over New Netherland in 1664 they offered citizenship to a population that spoke eighteen different languages.

Many of the two million white people inhabiting the colonies at the time of the Revolution were immigrants or the descendants of non-English stock. In addition, five hundred thousand free and slave Negroes lived in North America, mainly in the South. In every colony there was a variety of nationalities on the frontier. The British had appropriated coastal lands in the early years of settlement and later immigrants, most of them from the Continent, had to move farther inland. The colonies were eager to have settlements protecting them from attacks by Indians and Frenchmen and they were willing to subsidize frontiersmen to act as a buffer. Some Europeans came to the colonies specifically to take advantage of the land grants and other privileges offered to pioneers.

Despite their diversity, the thirteen colonies could claim an over-all cohesiveness by 1775. As founders and rulers the British

In the mid-1600's New York City resembled a Dutch village complete with windmills and canal. This scale model points up one important difference, however: New York also had a fort. CARL FRANK

set the standards which all later immigrants had to measure up to—or try to modify. Even in Pennsylvania, where they accounted for only one-third of the population—about the same as the Germans—Englishmen determined the language, laws and general customs of the colony. Presumably, *colonists* everywhere are free to establish their own patterns of life and those who come later, *immigrants,* must adjust to them. By that definition many American "colonists" were "immigrants," too, because they had to re-evaluate themselves according to a British model. The inner conflict they felt as old values clashed with new ones has characterized the Americanization process from the seventeenth century to the present.

Adherence to British customs and loyalty to the British Crown helped unify the diverse strains in colonial life. As in New England, intermarriage also played its part. In *Letters From An American Farmer,* the Frenchman, Hector St. John de Crèvecoeur answered the question, "What then is an American, this new man?" with this reply:

He is either an European, or the descendant of an European, hence that strange mixture of blood, which you will find in no other country. I could point out to you a family whose grandfather was an Englishman, whose wife was Dutch, whose son married a Frenchwoman, and whose present four sons have now four wives of different nations.

Cotton Mather, the fiery Puritan minister, was the first man on record, in 1684, to use the term an "American." Not long afterward this type was considered sufficiently distinctive to have "national" traits, most of which were fostered by frontier life. Colonists were thought to be more adaptable, independent and inventive than Europeans. They were also more devoted to democratic principles. Ownership of land was required for participation in government and, since frontier land was free or very cheap, men could easily become landowners and join in running the community. This inevitably led to that "disgusting equality" noted by an English visitor to the colonies.

Under Great Britain's "salutary neglect," Americans became far more dedicated to the rule of law than the rule of a king. For over one hundred years they governed themselves quite competently. Already self-reliant in government, the colonists became self-confident in military matters, as well, through the French and Indian Wars. They felt they had brought these sporadic outbreaks of fighting to a successful conclusion in 1763 without the help of the British Army or Navy. As "a people accustomed to more than British liberty" the colonists became angered when Great Britain tried to tighten its control over them in the second half of the eighteenth century.

When hostilities with Great Britain deepened, Americans of every background rallied to the defense of the colonies. A Negro seaman, Crispus Attucks, was one of the first to fall in the Boston Massacre of 1770 and Paul Revere alerted minutemen of both races on his famous ride in 1775. The following year fifty-six "Americans" signed the Declaration of Independence: eighteen were of non-English stock and eight were first-generation immigrants. George Washington counted men from every European group in his army, yet certain individuals of each nationality remained loyal to the British Crown. Men were Loyalists for a variety of reasons, not the least of which was self-preservation. Frontiersmen in Pennsylvania and Virginia remembered that the

Here, the Boston Massacre, one of the incidents
leading to the Revolutionary War. Hostilities with
Great Britain helped foster solidarity among
"Americans" of differing national origins and
religious affiliations. COURTESY OF THE
METROPOLITAN MUSEUM OF ART. GIFT OF
MRS. RUSSELL SAGE, 1910

British Army, not colonial militiamen, had saved them from Indian massacres and they did not want to lose its support for future emergencies.

◀ℓ "WHOM WE SHALL WELCOME"

The Revolutionary War fostered a romantic image of America as a haven for the oppressed of the world. In his Revolutionary tract, *Common Sense,* Thomas Paine called America "the asylum for the persecuted lovers of civil and religious liberty from every part of Europe." Philip Freneau, the poet, rejoiced in the establishment of the United States, a land to which the stranger could flee "from Europe's proud, despotic shores." George Washington's message to Irish immigrants in 1783 reiterates this theme:

The bosom of America is open to receive not only the opulent and respectable stranger, but the oppressed and persecuted of all Nations and Religions; whom we shall welcome to a participation of all our rights and privileges if, by decency and propriety of conduct, they appear to merit the enjoyment.

These lofty sentiments were quite a departure from the suspicion which had greeted most newcomers in the early days of the colonies. Belgians had been allowed to settle in Jamestown only on the condition that not more than three hundred enter and that they conform to the Church of England. At first Maryland would not allow any but English and Irish to own land and the Irish did not gain their political rights until 1674. Almost every colony did its best to discourage Catholics from immigrating, for their religion was considered a threat to the government. Consequently, Catholics were not eligible for the special land bounties and other subsidies offered to Protestant immigrants.

Throughout history times of crisis have evoked feelings of hostility toward foreigners and the French and Indian Wars proved no exception. Suddenly, colonists found their German neighbors to be dangerous and they violently harassed the "Dutchmen." Americans similarly mistreated French Huguenots because the latter originated in the same land as the enemy. Since the Protestant Huguenots had been driven from Catholic France on religious grounds, it was unlikely that in the New World they would have come to the aid of their oppressors. But, as will be seen time and again in subsequent periods of American history, prejudice is irrational.

Even as the new nation was being formed, some leaders expressed mixed emotions about immigration. Thomas Jefferson was torn between his love of liberty and his fear of Europe's corrupting influences. He wanted to welcome the victims of tyranny, but he didn't want them to ruin America, "warp and bias its direction, and render it a . . . distracted mass." Delegates to the Constitutional Convention reflected many shades of opinion on the subject. Some delegates wanted to open the door wide to immigrant legislators while others wanted to bar them from government altogether. One delegate said he was in favor of a liberal immigration policy, but he didn't want "to be governed by foreigners and adventurers." In its final form, the Constitution requires a naturalized citizen to reside in the United States for seven years after receiving his papers before he may be elected to the House of Representatives. The waiting period was lengthened by two years for the Senate. Only a natural-born citizen or an immigrant who had become a citizen before the Constitution was adopted could be elected President.

Congress made few laws dealing with immigration. It passed a quarantine law solely as a health precaution and required only five years of waiting before an alien, foreign-born resident could become a citizen. In 1788 it stopped the troublesome influx of convicts—which led Great Britain to found Australia as a true penal colony. White servitude was not dealt with by the early legislators, but public opinion was already shifting against the "traffick of White People" as being inconsistent with the ideals of liberty. Ironically, the first group to take advantage of American asylum were nobles fleeing the French Revolution. Their coming annoyed many ardent democrats who had just fought a long war to throw off the yoke of monarchy. In response to the popular mood of 1795, Congress required applicants for citizenship to renounce not only allegiance to their former homeland, but any titles of nobility they may have held.

The founders of the Republic dedicated the United States to the highest ideals of brotherhood. Nothing could be more stirring than these words from the Declaration of Independence:

We hold these truths to be self-evident, that all men are created equal, that they are endowed by their Creator with certain inalienable Rights, that among these are Life, Liberty, and the Pursuit of Happiness.

Yet we know from his subsequent career that Thomas Jefferson did not mean Negroes when he wrote "all men are created equal." The same men who saw a disparity between the ideals of democracy and convict and indentured labor condoned slavery. Indeed, they delayed for twenty years the final end of the slave trade although its horrors were well-known. The framers of the Constitution never referred to slaves directly. They said "all other persons" should count as three-fifths of a man for the purposes of taxation and representation. This squarely fixed the Negro slaves' position in society as personal property, something substantially less than a "man."

Americans thought Negroes would remain permanently apart from and inferior to the rest of society, but they fully expected white immigrants to blend into the population. They could not foresee the huge waves of immigration that would create minority groups, descendants of non-English immigrants who could not easily conform to an Anglo-American stereotype. But that would pose problems for future generations. In his classic letter to the Hebrew congregation of Newport in 1790, George Washington could say optimistically:

It is now no more that toleration is spoken of, as if it was by the indulgence of one class of people that another enjoyed the exercise of their inherent natural rights. For happily the Government of the United States, which gives to bigotry no sanction, to persecution no assistance, requires only that they who live under its protection should demean themselves as good citizens, in giving it on all occasions their effective support.

As conditions in Ireland worsened, farmers,
craftsmen and shopkeepers by the thousands
abandoned their homeland. Here, a priest gives his
blessings to the emigrants while friends and
relatives say goodbye. NEW YORK PUBLIC LIBRARY

Flight from Famine

AMERICA'S PROMISES OF WELCOME and equality were soon put to the test. Two hundred and fifty thousand Europeans sought out the new Republic between 1790 and 1815. With the growth of transatlantic shipping after that, immigrants arrived in undreamed of numbers: forty-two million to date. The Irish were the first to come en masse. Although their influx reached a peak in 1852, following the potato famine, it began years earlier in conjunction with trade.

୬୧ TRADE: The Key to Immigration

It was always easy for a rich European to get to America. He just picked the ship he wanted, paid his fare and crossed in a comfortable stateroom. But the peasant—and he was the typical immigrant—would have had to save a lifetime to finance a transatlantic voyage, and even then he probably would have gone into debt to pay the fare. In colonial times the indenture and redemptioner systems solved the problem. Later, it remained for commerce to provide transportation at a price the average European could afford.

Transatlantic trade began to expand after the Napoleonic Wars ended in 1815. The sea lanes were dotted with the billowing white sails of freighters carrying raw materials to Europe and finished goods to America. European factory workers transformed American lumber into furniture, woodenware and building materials. They took American tobacco and cotton and turned them into cigars and cloth. Merchants distributed the manufactured products throughout the Continent and exported them to the United States, which had not yet developed an extensive factory system.

The raw materials were heavier than the finished goods and there was always free space on westbound ships. This weight differential had led many ship captains into the slave and indentured servant trade in colonial times. When the importation of slaves was prohibited in 1808 and the indenture system ended, captains loaded their holds with ballast to keep their ships steady. But ballast brought in no money, so the traders began to cast around for a substitute that would. Immigrants were the ideal "cargo" since they loaded and unloaded themselves, shifted themselves in a storm and in an emergency could even be put to the bailing pumps! Since immigrants brought their own food, whatever they paid was pure profit. Thus, lacking any sense of historic purpose and desiring only to increase their wealth, traders began to encourage immigration, and immigrants in turn came to depend on merchant vessels for cheap transportation. As a result, immigration followed trade routes.

✐ WOOD

Once Ireland had been green with trees, but that time was now recalled only in legend. When Saxon invaders from England conquered the country in the twelfth century, they stripped the land of its forests and the name "Emerald Isle" came to refer only to Ireland's lush meadows. The laborers and cottiers—peasants who worked small plots of rented land—used dried turf for fuel instead of wood. They built their cottages of mud and stone, but they still needed wood for supporting beams. And as Ireland's population expanded, the demand for wood to be used in building and making barrels increased. By 1830 every seaport village in the south and west of the island had small boats going to Canada, where the forests grew right down to the shores of the St. Lawrence River.

Hoping to make extra money, the ship captains began to stir up interest in Canada. In time, there was so much competition among them for immigrant "cargo" that the fares dropped to just half of what it would cost an Irishman to sail to New York. The Canadian route had other advantages, too. The shorter trip meant that the traveler needed fewer supplies. The boats set out in the spring to pick up the winter's cuttings and spring was also the time when immigrants wanted to go to the New World. They had been advised to get established before the cold weather set in.

The newcomer to Canada's shores could get work immediately on the docks loading the timber fleet. The following winter he could find employment in one of the lumber camps in the nearby forests or in the shipyards along the waterfront. If he went inland there were jobs to be had on farms and road gangs, although one cruel winter in the Canadian forest was usually enough for any immigrant.

Hearing about opportunities in the United States, many immigrants who had taken advantage of the cheaper rates to Canada later turned their sights southward. There were more year-round jobs available in the States and land was easier to acquire. For some, the United States had always been their ultimate destination. They had just stayed in Canada long enough to earn some money before they headed south. Others arrived in the United States by chance; it was said that they just "fell over the line." A number of immigrants rode fertilizer boats down the coast. But for many poor Irishmen the simplest way to get to the States from Canada was to walk, and thousands did. Some Irishmen came from as far away as New Brunswick, working or begging their way through the Maine wilderness to large centers of employment, such as Boston. The captain of the ship *Ocean,* advertising a forthcoming voyage, pointed out: "Those living on that line of road being very kind to Strangers as they pass." Some immigrants remained in small communities along the way attracting Irish newcomers to their towns.

✌ CANALS

At the same time that the pioneer Irish were crossing into New England from Canada, the Emerald Isle was experiencing the effects of a population explosion that made it the most crowded country in Europe. To feed all the extra mouths, Ireland's land was divided and subdivided until almost half the holdings were between one and five acres and thousands of families survived on even less than that. Ambitious younger sons who would inherit no land and farmers and laborers who saw their situation worsening were intrigued with advertisements of opportunity in America. They heard of jobs from ship captains and read about them in local newspapers.

These advertisements were placed by American construction companies, particularly those engaged in building transportation facilities. Federal and state governments stood ready to spend great sums on roads, canals and, eventually, railroads to link Western supply regions with eastern seaboard markets. Yet construction companies could not find men to do the job. Manpower had been scarce in America since the founding of Jamestown, but it was becoming nonexistent as native men sought property of their own in the newly opened Western territories. In any case, American men simply would not do pick and shovel work, which they felt was beneath them. Faced with the problem of large projects and few workers, construction companies followed the example of colonial employers: they turned to Europe.

The Irishmen they recruited performed yeoman services in America. They excavated the foundations of mills, factories and homes, they constructed wharves and they loaded and unloaded supplies. Irishmen helped dig almost every American canal, and the famous Erie Canal was largely built with Irish muscle. By 1825 the Erie Canal linked the Great Lakes with New York City, establishing it as the greatest trading center in the country. Rates on the Erie Canal were so much cheaper than on other routes that people went out of their way to use it. Philadelphians, for example, were amazed to learn that the cheapest way for them to trade with Pittsburgh, a city in their own state, was to go through New York. To correct this situation, Pennsylvania constructed almost one thousand miles of canals in fifteen years. Many other states also built impressive canal systems, yet by 1860 most of them were obsolete. In the 1850's shippers made a dramatic switch to railroads, which were better suited to long hauls and could operate in icy weather when canals had to close.

Canal building was miserable work. The men often stood in dirty water all day, easy prey to serious diseases such as dysentery, cholera, malaria and typhus. Moreover, they were constantly threatened by slipping machinery and collapsing banks. Men who fell ill or were injured on the job had no insurance to help their families until they recovered. Of course, many never did recover and grave sites along the canal are still in evidence, as dramatic reminders of a harsher economic era.

The workers were also victimized by their bosses. Contractors advertised for larger crews than they needed and the resulting competition for jobs kept wages low. Moreover, companies refused to pay the men when it rained and they couldn't work. Even so, the canal wages of fifty cents to a dollar fifty a day were high in comparison to Ireland's salaries. When the immigrants wrote home about their incomes, fellow countrymen were encouraged to try the United States. In 1827 some twenty thousand Irish arrived here, while five years later that figure had jumped to over sixty-five thousand. This advance guard started a trend toward the United States, so that when the great potato famine devastated the Emerald Isle, it was toward America that so many victims looked for hope.

⤐ THE FAMINE

The *patata,* as the Spanish explorers called it, had been grown in America for centuries by the Indians. The potato was introduced to Europe by Sir Francis Drake in the late seventeenth century and within one hundred years it had become as necessary to the Europeans as rice to the Chinese. In Hirschhorn, Germany, there still stands a statue dedicated piously "To God and Francis Drake, who brought to Europe for the everlasting benefit of the poor—the Potato."

Four million of Ireland's nine million inhabitants depended almost solely on the potato for nourishment. They developed many ways of preparing it and, what they couldn't eat they fed to the family animals or used for thatching roofs. Women and children could tend the potato patch easily and they could extract large crops with little care. One variety of potato, the "lumper" even grew nicely on unfertilized land. The potato had other advantages in that it was not menaced by insect enemies and it stored well through the winter. Yet even in good times the potato crop of one year didn't last until the next crop could be harvested. In the summer months many poor families had to forage for weeds and nettles. Despite the bad effect the potato had on the soil, small farmers refused to diversify their crops. The potato had saved them from famine on several occasions and the peasants remained steadfastly loyal to it.

Despite Ireland's chronic economic troubles, many people found reason to be encouraged in the summer of 1845. The island's exports of wheat and pork were selling well in Great Britain and the potato crop promised to be lush. No one suspected that Ireland would soon be the victim of the worst national disaster since the bubonic plague in the fourteenth century.

The "potato disease" was first identified in Germany in 1829. It attacked some part of that country every season thereafter. In 1844 North America was stricken with the potato blight and the following year all Europe was hit hard by it. Ireland had suffered scattered blights before, but nothing severe enough to discourage replanting. However, the mysterious rot of 1845 cost the island between one-third and one-half its normal crop and this time the fungus killed the potatoes in storage as well as the potatoes in the ground.

During the first winter after the blight struck, many Irishmen were saved by neighborly kindness, private British charity and government relief. The following spring the people watched the potato crop anxiously. They had lived through one year of shortage before, but they knew they could not survive two blight years in a row. Although early conditions looked good, the crop failed again.

Some said that it took a few days to kill the potatoes; others held that the rot of '46 set in overnight. On his way from Cork to

Dublin that summer Father Matthew commented on the healthy potato crop. When he retraced his steps one week later all he saw was "one wide waste of putrefying vegetation. In many places the wretched people were seated on the fences of their decaying gardens, wringing their hands and wailing bitterly the destruction that had left them foodless." The potato failure was probably no worse than that of the year before, but now there was no reserve food to draw on.

Had Ireland alone been the victim of crop failures, all of Europe would have come to her aid. But troubled by shortages of their own, foreign countries could not afford such charity. The British, who governed Ireland, bent their energies toward marshalling private support for the famine victims. While the British did send a great deal of food across the Irish Sea, it was not enough to feed an entire population. To this day many Irishmen harbor resentment against the British for misgovernment during the famine crisis. Americans quickly raised one million dollars, a very large sum in those days, to outfit relief ships.

Ireland's troubles were not over when food supplies arrived in winter. By that time the island's rivers were frozen, there were not enough horses and carts to carry the food inland, and there was no alternate means of transportation. Moreover, the Irish had raised wheat for export only. When the grain was shipped back to the island, the people didn't know how to make bread nor did they have ovens in which to bake it! The problems of transportation and food preparation were eventually overcome, and many people survived through the help of soup kitchens which ladled out mush made from American corn.

Unfortunately, relief came too late for many Irish peasants. Some people simply accepted their fate, shutting themselves up in their cottages to die. Others took to the road, begging and stealing whatever they could get to stay alive. These hungry wanderers spread the deadly "famine fever," a form of typhus that claimed the lives of many who escaped actual starvation. Finally, there were too many corpses for proper burial and many famine victims were just placed in pits, their names unrecorded. In all, five hundred thousand died. As Lord Mountcashell, an Irish landlord, told the commander of an American relief ship:

It would be an endless task, as well as a most painful one, to note down the details of individual suffering. Every day furnishes victims, and the living hear, and endeavor to drive from their minds, as soon as they can, the horrifying particulars that are related. I have this day, returning to my house, witnessed more than one person dying by the road side. I have been informed that there are dead bodies lying in our district at this moment unburied. I have known of bodies here remaining in the mountainous parts, neglected for more than eight days; and I am at this time giving food to a girl of twelve years old, the only remnant of a family, consisting of eight persons, her father and mother included, all of whom were alive one fortnight ago. Need I say more to rouse your sympathy?

The potato blight completely disrupted the economic life of Ireland. Pigs and chickens were slaughtered for food or else they died for lack of potato scraps to eat. Thus, men who had made a living collecting and marketing pork and eggs were put out of work. Since people bought only what they absolutely needed, trade dwindled to nothing and small shopkeepers and craftsmen became beggars alongside their former customers.

Priests, too, were desperate because their parishioners could not contribute toward their support. All those whose lives were somehow involved with the potato farmer went down with him.

↩ THE ESCAPE

Before the famine, Irishmen had thought of emigration as exile, but now they welcomed it as the only alternative to death. Even many Catholic priests who had formerly advised parishioners to stay home near their churches began urging them to leave. Once the Irish decided to abandon their country, not even improving conditions could change their minds. The idea was widely held that a curse rested upon the land. "Poor Ireland's done. It can never again recover," emigrants said wherever they gathered. The peak year of the exodus was 1852, but Irishmen continued to leave in large numbers for years afterwards. By 1864 some two and a half million had come to the United States and by 1929 that figure had soared to four and a half million. As recently as 1956–65, over seventy thousand Irish immigrated to America.

At the time of the famine the British inadvertently spurred emigration from Ireland. By repealing the corn laws in 1846, the British removed Ireland's favored status in the British marketplace. Unable to compete with mass producers such as the Americans, small Irish landowners decided to emigrate. Those large landowners who switched from wheat growing to cattle raising as a result of repeal threw cottiers off their land so they could use it as pasture. Many of these evicted peasants, too, emigrated. With passage of the "poor law" in 1847, the British disqualified ten-

In the 1840's many Americans were becoming
concerned about the growing influx of Irishmen.
Some natives vented their hostility in mob
violence such as the anti-immigrant riot pictured
here. LIBRARY OF CONGRESS

acre Irish landlords from poor relief. The British thought these farmers would give up their land and become agricultural workers in order to obtain relief funds. But the Irish did not want to be servants where they had once been masters, so they sold their land and emigrated. Another provision in the law stated that middle-income farmers had to support the poor. Rather than see their profits drained away each year in poor relief, this group, too, departed. "The poor law is the great and permanent depopulator of Ireland," declared an editorial in the *King's County Chronicle*.

At first glance it seems amazing that people on the brink of starvation could finance a transatlantic voyage, yet in fact many people had access to several sources of money. Often their thatched roofs contained a few dollars saved for an emergency. The sale of furniture brought in a little more. Some poor people begged for their passage and many used what should have been last year's rent to pay the fare. Bank notes from relatives in the United States and Canada which were intended for relief at home were used for the best "relief" the Irish knew—escape. In many instances landlords paid for several passages and a few even chartered ships to carry their tenants away. Some landlords acted out of kindness, but others felt this was cheaper than supporting paupers at home.

The cheapest place for the peasants to go was England, for the day's sail over the Irish Sea cost only seventy or eighty cents. Many Irishmen were familiar with England from having worked there during the harvest season. After the blight thousands of famine refugees landed in cities along the English and Welsh coast looking for permanent homes. In 1847 more than a quarter of a million reached the city of Liverpool alone. Some of these emigrants eventually moved on to the United States or Canada, but many remained in the great industrial cities of northern England where their descendants live today.

Thousands of the poorest famine victims left Ireland in the awkward timber boats headed for Canada, because that trip still cost less than passage to the United States. The ships were not outfitted for passengers, so the emigrants had to camp out as best they could in the empty space below decks. When they boarded the ships, the peasants rejoiced that they had left suffering behind. But in the dirty, packed steerage—the cheapest quarters—the passengers suffered attacks of "ship's fever," a violent form of hunger typhus. Some had been sick with it before they came on board, while others carried the germ in the lice-infested clothing they had salvaged from the bodies of dead people. The Canadian government tried to prevent the typhus epidemic from spreading inland by holding the fever victims in quarantine. The makeshift stations it set up were inadequate, however, and in 1847 some ten thousand died in one such quarantine area alone.

Inadequate quarantine facilities, the high accident rate on the crude timber ships and Canada's new immigration tax led more and more Irishmen to board the cotton ships leaving Liverpool for the United States. Moreover, the cotton ship owners wooed immigrants by offering free trips across the Irish Sea. Although the ships loaded in southern American ports, they dropped anchor first in northern cities to unload British wares and passengers. The immigrants preferred to debark in the North, where they could find work more readily than in the South. Another reason why the Irish were particularly eager to travel the

A newly arrived immigrant being set upon by
"runners," unscrupulous men who made a practice
of cheating greenhorns as they stepped off the boat.

Liverpool–United States route was that American ships made
that journey, whereas they almost never called at Irish ports.
American ships enjoyed a fine reputation and even the British,
who were renowned for their naval prowess, admitted that the
American skipper was better than his English counterpart. American captains either owned their ships or had been carefully
chosen to meet the high standards of American companies insur-
ing the cargoes. "Let the ship be American," advised the most
widely read emigrant guidebook, "remember he is going home,
and the captain probably will never pull off his clothes to go to
bed during the whole voyage."

Forty days after boarding ship at Liverpool, the immigrants landed in the New World. They were strange in manners and shabby in dress. Dazed by the sights and sounds of the New World, many were cheated by dishonest people of their own stock who made a business out of tricking newcomers. These "runners" swarmed around the docks looking for innocent green-horns just off the boat. Speaking Gaelic, the historic language of Ireland, or English with an Irish brogue, they offered to get the newcomers rooms, transportation and jobs—all at outrageous prices. Various organizations such as the Irish Emigrant Society of New York tried to protect their countrymen, but they had neither the money nor the authority to do so. In 1846 a committee investigating conditions for new arrivals in New York was shocked at the amount of fraud practiced upon immigrants. It found "the German preying upon the German—the Irish upon the Irish—the English upon the English." The following year

In 1855 New York State set up an immigrant reception center at Castle Garden. Here for the first time newcomers could obtain information, change money and arrange for transportation without harassment from "runners."
NEW YORK PUBLIC LIBRARY

New York state, which received most of the newcomers, set up a board of immigration. By 1855 it had established an immigrant depot at Castle Garden—at various times a fort and an opera house—near the tip of Manhattan. Here, immigrants could exchange foreign money, arrange for rooms, buy railroad tickets and ask about jobs without fear of being cheated.

✑ TEXTILES AND TRANSPORTATION

On the whole the famine refugees were unskilled and illiterate and some spoke only Gaelic. Since most of them knew only elementary farming, they had to start out in America doing the most menial work. For a time most immigrants stayed in the cities where they landed—they were too poor to go anywhere else. They needed jobs right away, and American cities, which were in their infancy, needed men to pave streets, dig sewers, lay gas and water pipes and build houses. The young Irish men, who usually came first, lived frugally, saving every possible cent to bring over their fathers, then the rest of their families. The women found jobs as cooks, nurses and maids, earning anywhere from one dollar to a few dollars a week plus room and board. By 1855 one quarter of New York City's Irish workers were laborers, carters, porters and waiters. Another quarter were domestic servants and 10 per cent worked as tailors and dressmakers.

Many Irishmen who gravitated toward New England found employment in the area's expanding textile industry. At first the Irish helped construct hundreds of new cotton and woolen mills there. When they had finished, some of the men began to work inside the buildings as janitors and then as machine operators. At the machines they stood next to the American farm girls who were the mills' original employees. The girls thought of factory work as a means of earning a dowry before settling down on farms of their own. But when the Irishmen moved into the mills, the girls began to leave. They didn't want to be associated with the foreigners, whom they considered beneath them socially. The girls' departure was hastened by factory owners who began to cut salaries when they saw that the Irish would work for less money. The owners had been required to provide respectable boarding houses and strict moral supervision for the young ladies, whereas the Irish provided their own housing and required no chaperones. By 1860 almost all the factory hands in New England mills were Irish. Later, they would be replaced by newer immigrant groups, such as the French Canadians.

The transportation industry also provided work for thousands of Irishmen, who were the backbone of the railroads as they had been of the canals. The Irishmen graded the road beds, laid the rails and drove the spikes. They performed dangerous tasks, too, such as setting dynamite to blast through solid rock. Sometimes the dynamite went off before they could scramble away and many men died in the explosions.

After the Civil War many Irishmen went to work on the Union Pacific Railroad, which met the Central Pacific in 1869 to link the two coasts. The men often had to drop their sledge hammers and quickly pick up their rifles to ward off Indian attacks. So many Irish died while building the Union Pacific that the

Irish workers contributed greatly to the development of America's vast transportation network. First the immigrants dug the canals and then they helped lay the railroad tracks that spanned a continent. MINNESOTA HISTORICAL SOCIETY

saying went, "There's an Irishman buried under every tie." One of America's folk songs, "Poor Paddy, He Works on the Railroad," recalls those days:

> Then drill my Paddies, drill—
> Drill, my heroes drill,
> Drill all day, no sugar in your tay,
> Working on the U.P. railway.

Irish workers were exploited as much on the railroads as they had been on the canals. The men were supposed to get $1.25 a day, but time after time their bosses—many of them fellow Irishmen—made off with their salaries. Labor contractors ignored any demands for better conditions or higher wages, even refusing to grant the fifteen-cent-a-day increase one group struck for. After working from sunrise until their "sweat mixed with the nightly dew," as one worker put it, the laborers had little to show for their efforts. They had to buy food and clothes at the overpriced company store, which kept them in debt. With no organized way to protest, the workers often took out their anger in what were called "Irish riots" and on several occasions state militia were summoned to prevent them from ripping out work they had just finished.

Conditions were little better in the coal industry, where many Irishmen sought employment after manning railroad crews. The men went to dig in the coalfields of western Pennsylvania, eastern Kentucky and what is now West Virginia. Some of the Irishmen had learned about mining during a stay in England, but most of them were complete novices. The coal mining companies would not recognize the employees' right to bargain collectively. Unable to unionize, some men formed a secret terror organization called the Molly Maguires. Like the "Irish riots" on the railroads, the Molly Maguires gave Irishmen—and all immigrants— a reputation for violence in labor that was largely undeserved. Finally the Irish made a breakthrough and organized the workers into unions. Today every contract the coal miners accept includes a holiday on the birthday of James Mitchell, the Irish labor leader.

The Irishmen's work took them to every state. When canal and railroad gangs broke up, the men put their picks and shovels on their backs and went looking for other jobs. Some of the immigrants settled down on farms near the railroads they had helped to build. But most went back to the cities where wives and children awaited their return.

By the nineteenth century people all over the world had started to move from country to city. Although the population of Ireland decreased by two and a half million between 1841 and 1861, the population of every large city on the island increased markedly during the same period. In America the lure of the city was stronger than the promise of available land in the West, even during the period of our greatest westward expansion.

Irish immigrants settled in port cities at first because they didn't hàve the money to move on or to purchase farms. But, even when they could afford to leave, most Irishmen preferred the city to the country. The failure of the land had been the reason they had left home in the first place. Why should they overlook certain wages in construction and factory work to chance everything on the land again? The Irish were devout Catholics, for the most part, and they didn't want to move too far from a church of their faith. Moreover, rural America was a lonely place. As one Irish-American farmer compared his old and new homes:

I could then go to a fair, or a wake, or a dance . . . I could spend the winter's night in a neighbor's house cracking jokes by the turf fire. If I had there but a sore head I would have a neighbor within every three hundred yards of me that would run to see me. But here everyone can get so much land . . . that they calls them neighbors that live three miles off.

Irish immigrants crowded into the first of the countless miserable slums America would come to know. They threw together shantytowns of discarded boxes and timbers on vacant lots near factories or on the outskirts of towns. In cities their lodgings were described as "the oldest, most rickety buildings, open to the wind and storm and far less comfortable than the buildings used as barns or cattle stalls by the great body of farmers throughout the country." These tenements were breeding grounds for all kinds of diseases, and an observer noted that in the worst neighborhoods no one lived to have gray hairs. One statistician estimated that the Irish in Boston survived only about fourteen years after landing here. On the other hand, in nineteenth-century Ireland the average age at death was nineteen, and four-fifths of the population did not reach the age of forty.

The immigrants worked hard to free themselves and their children from shantytowns and "Little Dublins." Under the guidance of the Democratic Party many Irishmen advanced themselves through city government. They started out as minor party officials, known as "ward heelers." In their precincts, or wards, they found jobs for new arrivals, bailed out petty offenders, sent flowers to funerals and gave Christmas dinners to the poorest residents. From ward heelers some men rose to positions as city councilmen and even mayors. Although the Irish were blamed for corruption in city politics, in most instances the immigrants were following the orders of native Americans who controlled the party machines.

Irishmen went to work for city governments in many capacities. Immigrants could join the police force immediately because United States citizenship and a literacy test were not generally a requirement until after 1859. Irishmen could work themselves up through the ranks and, after the Civil Service system was widely adopted, they had the advantage of job security. The uniforms, parades and element of danger in a policeman's life seemed glamorous to many poor immigrants. So many Irish-Americans served as policemen that the vans that transported prisoners became known as "paddy wagons."

The Irishman also became a familiar figure in city fire departments. Being a fireman held many of the same attractions as being a policeman. Some immigrant firemen started out as amateurs because all city fire fighting was in the hands of volunteer companies before the Civil War. (In those days, a fire alarm was often the signal for general uproar. Fire companies would send their fastest runners to secure the one hydrant in the area while they brought out their gleaming "machines." Fights between rival volunteer groups frequently broke out over which one would have the honor of fighting the fire—all the while a building could be burning to the ground!) Many other Irishmen became street cleaners and street car operators.

Living together in the city, the Irish found it relatively easy to organize volunteer activities, such as fire fighting and military drilling. Volunteer drilling units were popular before the Civil War, but immigrants were not welcomed into the military organizations of native Americans. If immigrants wanted to drill, they had to form their own groups, and every foreign-born community of any size boasted several brigades. The Irish served their units with gusto; during the Civil War, many of the members marched off to war together.

Irishmen also lent their talents to the development of American Catholicism, which originally consisted of a small organization headed by French-Canadian clergymen. The Irish, who introduced the English language to the Church here, contributed many priests, bishops and charity leaders. Largely as a result of the newcomers' efforts, the Catholic Church became well-established and today it is the largest unified religious organization in the United States. Irishmen also started the parochial school system which has educated the offspring of immigrants from many countries. Their preparatory schools and colleges, such as Villanova, Fordham and Georgetown Universities, have contributed much to American education. Although in any one year more Polish or German names may be found in the line-up, the football players of Notre Dame are still referred to as the "fighting Irish."

THE KNOW-NOTHINGS

Despite their contributions to America, Irishmen met with prejudice and discrimination. Every new group suffered hostility here, but the Irish may have had the worst time of all because they were the first really large group to come over. Americans, who associated Europeans with crime, poverty and moral decadence, became fearful of being "overrun" by the Irish. Moreover, the Irish were Catholic and the Protestant American prejudice against that religion, present in colonial times, was still prevalent.

Irishmen were often criticized for being stupid and lazy. Native farmers complained that their immigrant helpers did not want to work, when often the men were only awaiting specific instructions. American housewives condemned their Irish cooks for not being able to prepare meat. And no wonder—many of them had not seen meat from one year to the next at home. Americans were quick to point out that the Irish applied for relief, were arrested for petty stealing and had to be hospitalized more often than natives. Rather than rightfully attributing the immigrants' troubles to their extreme poverty, Americans assumed there was something inherently wrong with the group. Although this attack was leveled in 1868, it represents the feelings of many Americans in the decade before the Civil War:

Teddy O'Flaherty votes. He has not been in the country six months. He never knew an hour in civilized society. . . . Breaking heads for opinion's sake is his practice . . . pushed straight to hell by that abomination against common sense called the Catholic religion . . . The Irish fill our prisons, our poor houses. . . . Scratch a convict or a pauper, and the chances are that you tickle the skin of an Irish Catholic.

As more and more Irishmen arrived, employment barriers began to go up. Advertisements like these appeared in newspapers of the day:

CARPENTER—Skilled or unskilled for furniture shop. No Irish need apply.

WOMAN WANTED—To do all-around housework . . . English, Scotch, German or any country or color except Irish.

The Irish also met cruel social discrimination, particularly in New England. A large percentage of the immigrants had settled in that region because of the Canadian timber trade. Puritanical New Englanders were shocked to see Irishmen drinking whiskey on payday, which was Saturday night and a part of the holy Sabbath to them. They developed a theory that the Irishman's troubles could all be traced to drunkenness. Traditionally hostile to any newcomers, most New Englanders turned their backs on the Irish. In Boston, Yankee children were not allowed to eat or play with Irish children. In nearby Cambridge, two horsecar lines ran parallel to one another: one carried proper gentlemen to business and the other took Irish laborers and washerwomen to their jobs. Native parents told their children that Irish servant girls came from "a mysterious green island far across the sea . . . bringing many strange customs with them."

Taking advantage of ignorance and fear, local secret societies began to advance the slogan "America for Americans" in the 1840's. Eventually these groups merged into the Order of the Star-Spangled Banner. In 1854 the organization became nationally prominent under a new name, the American Party or, as it was commonly referred to, the Know-Nothing Party. The group got its nickname from the phrase, "I know nothing," which members were supposed to reply in response to questions about the party's activities. The Know-Nothings claimed that the Irish were stealing jobs from native workers and lowering wages. They warned of secret Catholic ceremonies and papal control of America. The Know-Nothings sought to restrict immigration, hinder naturalization and curb the growth of the Catholic Church.

As a result of Know-Nothing agitation, terrible destructive riots flared in several cities. Mobs attacked Catholic churches and assaulted nuns and priests. In 1855 Know-Nothing candidates captured six state governorships and seventy-five Congressional seats. The following year their candidate for President won 25

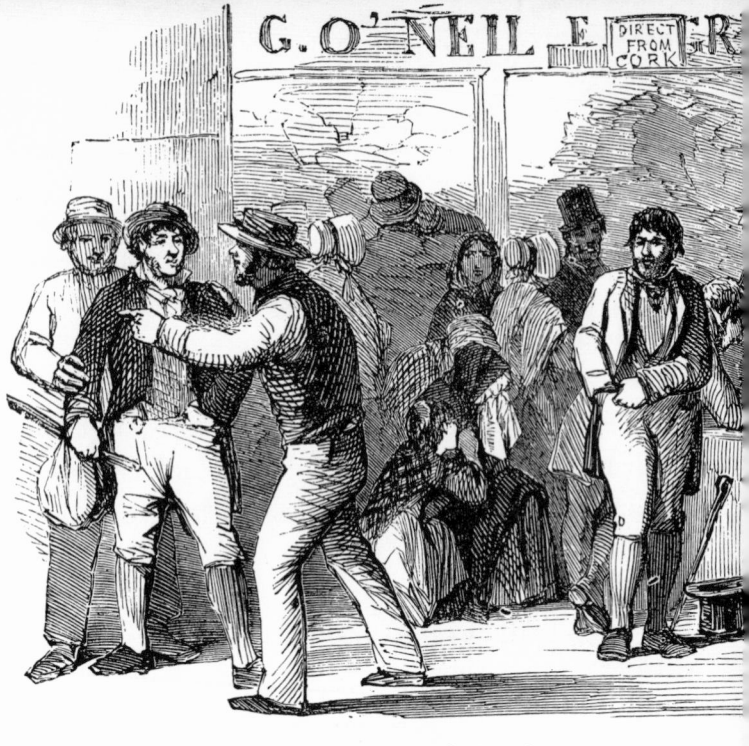

Booking passage on an emigrant ship. Irishmen fleeing the potato famine often sailed to England because the short trip over there cost less than a dollar. Others went to the United States and Canada.
NEW YORK PUBLIC LIBRARY

per cent of the vote. Despite these indications of widespread support, the Know-Nothing movement was short-lived because members disagreed on the major issue of the day: slavery.

THE CIVIL WAR

After 1854 thousands of Americans joined the new Republican Party. It was opposed to extending slavery to new territories and many of its followers wanted to free slaves in the South as well. Most Irishmen opposed this platform and remained loyal to the Democratic Party. Many were against liberating the slaves for

[66]

economic reasons: Irishmen knew that freed Negroes would compete with them for unskilled jobs, the only work open to them. As it was, Irishmen vied with freed Negroes for construction work and Irish women competed with Negro women for jobs as domestic servants and hotel employees.

Although Irishmen were against freeing the slaves, one hundred seventy thousand of them (including thousands of volunteers) fought for the North. Green flags with the harp and shamrock were present alongside the Stars and Stripes in almost every major battle. The Fifteenth Michigan Infantry was called the "Mulligan Regiment" and the Seventy-fifth of New York was called the "Irish Rifles." "The Irish spirit of the North is thoroughly aroused," rejoiced the *New York Tribune,* and no group was sent off to battle with more parades and celebrations.

By 1863 the spirit of volunteering was waning in the North and a national draft of soldiers had to be instituted to fill the Union ranks. The draft was extremely unpopular with newly arrived foreigners, many of whom had left Europe to escape military service. They felt the law was particularly unfair to poor people like themselves who could neither hire a substitute nor pay three hundred dollars to avoid military service.

The first drawing of draftees' names was the signal for the start of violence. The Germans who had settled in Milwaukee rioted, and largely Irish mobs held New York in a state of siege for three days. They looted stores and houses, lynched or tortured Negroes and robbed horse-car passengers. One half-crazed group burned down a Negro orphan asylum housing two hundred children between the ages of two and twelve. While many Irish policemen, firemen and priests acted nobly to control the mobs, many people felt the draft riots left a stain on Irish valor in the Civil War.

About forty thousand Irishmen fought for the Confederacy, reflecting the smaller immigrant population in the South. They tried to compete with the Union in recruiting soldiers in Ireland, but they couldn't offer the same generous bounties for army service.

IRISH NATIONALISM

When the Union forces disbanded, every soldier carried away the rifle with which he had fought. Many native Americans later put the guns to use opening up the frontier. But some Irishmen hoped to employ their weapons against the British.

Irishmen at home and in America bitterly resented the British, who ruled the island, and anti-British sentiment became the unifying bond for everyone of Irish descent. Irish leaders blamed the British for every one of the island's ills, harking back to their mismanagement of the potato famine and even earlier issues. Some Irish-Americans became so aroused by their leaders' passionate oratory that they enlisted in the Union Army merely to gain the military skill to fight the British.

After the Civil War an Irish Nationalist group called the Fenian Brotherhood decided to set up an "Irish Republic" in Canada to which Canadian Irishmen would flock and which the United States would quickly recognize. Fenians in Cincinnati drew up the plans and began to sell bonds for the new "Republic." On June 1, 1866, some fifteen hundred Fenians crossed the Niagara border, took Fort Erie and threw up entrenchments to protect themselves. After several minor skirmishes, however, the movement collapsed. Many Fenians were arrested, but eventually they were paroled and sent home at Government expense. The Administration of Andrew Jackson did not want to antagonize Irish-American voters by imposing harsh penalties on the invaders. In 1870 another attempted invasion of Canada was foiled by American and Canadian officials. When the news broke that the radical Clan-na-Gael planned to blow up British warships visiting New York harbor, many Americans worried about the strong bonds Irishmen felt with their ancestral country. They joined a disillusioned Irish-American leader in asking what would come of having an "alien population, camped but not settled in

Although the odds were against it, some Irishmen who arrived in America completely penniless did amass enough money to be able to return triumphantly to the "Ould Sod."
CHICAGO HISTORICAL SOCIETY

America, with foreign hopes and aspirations unshared by the people among whom they live."

As the years went on the Irish in America did not forget the "Ould Sod." Indeed, some second-generation Americans became even more devoted to the Emerald Isle than their fathers had been. Before America entered World War I, many Irishmen expressed pro-German sympathies. It wasn't that they admired Germans particularly, but they wanted to hurt the British, who were at war with them. Once the United States entered the war, however, the Irish gave this country their loyal support.

In December of 1921 the Anglo-Irish treaty created the Irish Free State, which gave Ireland dominion status in the British Commonwealth. When Ireland acquired complete independence in 1923, "professional Irishmen" in America turned their interests elsewhere and the close Irish associations across the Atlantic began to fade. Now that she was independent, Ireland was on her own.

Since new settlers were the lifeblood of western shipping, railroads expended a great deal of energy in attracting people to the frontier. This advertisement even appeals to the fainthearted by asserting, in fine print, that "the Indians have been removed." CHICAGO AND NORTH WESTERN RAILWAY

Farmers and Revolutionaries

THE GERMANS STARTED TO COME TO America in large numbers about the same time as the Irish. But whereas Irish immigration slackened after the Civil War, the German influx did not let up until the twentieth century. In all, six million Germans settled in the United States, more than any other incoming group. Most of them were "pushed" out of their homeland by worsening economic and social conditions.

UPHEAVAL IN GERMANY

In the first half of the nineteenth century, Germany, like Ireland, strained to support its increasing population. Farms were divided and subdivided until land was virtually torn into shreds. The only way families could survive on these small plots was by raising potatoes. "Potatoes are half the life of Germany, the foundation of peace and of the people's well-being" commented one observer. When the mysterious potato rot devastated Ireland and other parts of Europe in the 1840's, it crippled the German economy as well. Coming at the same time as other crop failures, the potato disease drove thousands of German peasants to sell their lands and depart for the New World. Other farmers who left before and after the rot went out in search of more land.

German craftsmen, too, found their economic situation deteriorating. As the Industrial Revolution gained momentum, automation took away more and more of their work. Machines used on an assembly line turned out products faster and more cheaply than master craftsmen could by working at home with simple tools. Finding themselves with a dwindling number of customers, spinners, weavers and other artisans went to the cities to find factory work. Thousands more used the proceeds from the sale of their equipment and cottages to finance a trip to America.

Germany's economic instability was matched by its volatile social atmosphere, which caused hundreds of thousands to emigrate. Until 1870, the Germans were united only by a common language, culture and ancient geographical designation. "Germany" really consisted of several separate states ruled by petty princes, but many Germans dreamed of uniting these states under a constitutional government. Soon after the beginning of the nineteenth century, Napoleon conquered and occupied the land, disrupting every facet of German life. The people rallied to oust the French forces and, during the ensuing struggle, the German princes promised their subjects a more democratic society. This promise was never fulfilled, however. The downfall of Napoleon in 1815 brought on a wave of reaction that made censorship of the press, repression of civil rights and police surveillance the rule of the day.

Out of sight of the government spies, students and others worked to unify and liberalize Germany. They staged several uprisings—all of them unsuccessful—and the revolutionaries who escaped jail were forced to emigrate. When Bismarck finally succeeded in unifying the country in 1870 he brought on a mass exodus. People wanted to avoid his harsh military rule and the Franco-Prussian War he launched the same year. Still thousands more left throughout the century to escape the mutual harassment Catholics and Protestants inflicted upon one another. As the British periodical, *Chambers' Edinburgh Journal,* viewed German emigration in 1846:

The one great cause of this almost national movement is the desire for absolute political and religious freedom. . . . The great agitation in society, caused first by the French domination, and then by the convulsive rise against it, has never passed away. . . . The young, the restless, and the imaginative thirst for their ideal freedom, and many of them seek for the realization of Utopia in America.

Despite their troubles and longings, most early nineteenth century German emigrants probably would have stayed home had not businessmen thought it profitable to transport them to the New World. Just as the lumber trade stimulated emigration from Ireland, cotton and tobacco primed the pump of German emigration.

◆ COTTON AND TOBACCO

Sometime after the fall of Napoleon, the hilly region of Alsace between France and Germany began to develop a cotton-manufacturing industry. America's southern states provided the cotton, which was unloaded at Le Havre on the west coast of France and then shipped overland to the textile mills. Like the timber merchants, cotton traders wanted to make extra money by filling their westbound ships with human cargo. They found few customers in France, for that country had lost too many men in the Napoleonic Wars to permit a wholesale exodus of her sons. Those Frenchmen who did emigrate went mainly to French-speaking regions in Canada. But the ships leaving Le Havre did not go empty, because the merchants found many Germans eager to sail to the United States. With the encouragement of agents, the Germans began to take steamboats, freight wagons and footpaths to Le Havre. In time so many German immigrants flocked to the French port that it looked and sounded like a German city.

The immigrant ships headed straight for New Orleans, the center of the cotton trade, but the Germans did not stay there long. These Northern Europeans were not accustomed to the hot, damp climate of the South, nor could they compete with slave labor for work. They quickly continued their voyage up the Mississippi River by steamboat. The steamers were truly a bargain in transportation, costing an immigrant only two dollars to move himself and all his baggage from New Orleans to Cincinnati, where a large community of his countrymen lived. The Mississippi River became a great highway for the Germans who entered the United States on cotton boats.

When merchants from the German city of Bremen saw the success of Le Havre in the cotton trade, they decided to attempt a similar commercial alliance with the United States. They chose to deal in tobacco because it was quickly becoming one of America's most popular exports to Europe. So many Germans became fond of smoking that one American official stationed abroad was prompted to remark, "Smoking is a natural want to the Germans." The Bremen merchants went to Baltimore, then the chief port for Maryland and Virginia tobacco, where they studied the business with great thoroughness. When they finished, they paid the planters and returned to Bremen with the leaves, which they manufactured into cigars or packaged for use in pipes. American planters were delighted to deal with the Germans because they offered cash on the spot instead of asking for credit. The planters gave them more and more of their stock until the merchants were handling half the tobacco export of the United States.

To facilitate their new trade, the Bremen merchants had the port of Bremerhaven built on the Baltic Sea. By 1833 ships bound for America were leaving the port on the first and fifteenth of each month. At first the Germans had been skeptical about the value of the immigrant trade, but now they eagerly sought out passengers to fill the empty holds of the westbound tobacco ships. Starting with big cities, they soon had agents covering small villages as well. One newspaper complained that Germany was "caught in a net of Bremen agents." In the early years the travelers were often sent to Baltimore, but the immigrants found little opportunity for work there and most continued their westward journey over the Cumberland Gap and on to the upper Mississippi Valley. Later, most Germans were routed to the bustling port of New York on the Hudson. Bremerhaven became known as "Der Vorort New Yorks"—the suburb of New York.

❧ THE VOYAGE

When a German finally succumbed to the enticements of a shipping agent and purchased his ticket for the United States, he immediately asked, "How do I get to the sea?" He found out that no matter what route he took, he was usually faced with a long, tiring trip. The well-to-do could travel pleasantly by fast stage coaches and spend their evenings relaxing in cozy inns. But such luxury was far beyond the means of the ordinary immigrant. He had to walk or ride in a slow covered wagon, camping out at night beside a small fire. Often there was a delay at the seaport, where unfavorable winds might detain a ship for several days. In the interim the immigrant wasted—or was cheated of—precious money. When the winds and tides were just right, the captain announced they would set sail and the immigrant scrambled aboard.

"But surely this isn't where I am to sleep!" he cried out in dismay as he viewed the dark, cramped hole that would be his home for the next two months. The agent had promised him an iron bed with clean sheets. Here were just temporary crude shelves where immigrants were jammed in suffocating layers. Sometimes ships were so crowded that passengers had to sleep in the stairways or in hastily constructed shacks on the top deck. As the voyage got underway, it became clear that the crowded conditions had more serious effects than mere discomfort. Cholera and smallpox often broke out and, even when there were no epidemics, the passengers often suffered scurvy and body ulcers from the close quarters. In 1847 Congress passed a law to remedy the over-crowding, but it was often ignored. So many died on immigrant ships that in 1853 the New York *Journal of Commerce* could still refer to them as "damned plague ships and swimming coffins."

The steerage quarters were most miserable during the storms that buffeted every sailing ship in the course of its long Atlantic voyage. Few immigrants had ever been to sea before and they were terrified by the groaning ropes and boards, the shrieking winds and the slapping waves. Passengers screamed or prayed, while others lay in bed, too seasick to move. After surviving the terrible ordeal of a storm, passengers were glad to rush up on deck when it subsided. One immigrant described the scene this way:

The passengers turned out on deck like bees in Spring. Some stand about the stove, cook, or wait their turn at the fire. Others take a walk around the jolly-boat, which I may call the ship's farmyard, and talk to the cow, or sheep, or pigs, or poultry in their several tongues; or, they sit upon the water-barrels amusing themselves with a book, or, by the aid of tobacco fumes, wonder what sort of a world it is they are bound for, and build castles in the air.

As the days stretched into weeks, boredom hung in the air like a damp, gray cloud. The cramped quarters and lack of activity on board often led to fights among the passengers. Sometimes captains took away all guns and imposed evening curfews to keep the situation under control. After the tedious weeks at sea,

Dinner in the steerage quarters. Overcrowding and crude facilities often made mealtimes aboard an immigrant ship very unpleasant, especially when a storm was brewing. THE METROPOLITAN MUSEUM OF ART, HARRIS BRISBANE DICK FUND, 1928

passengers and crew alike hailed the appearance of the New-foundland Banks. The fisheries meant that New York could not be far away. Often captains anchored their ships for a day or two to allow the passengers to catch halibut with improvised rods. The fishing provided a welcome change of activity as well as some diversification for the standard shipboard diet of salt meat and potatoes.

After the Civil War steamships began to ply the Atlantic on a regular basis. At first they were too expensive for the ordinary immigrant, but by 1870 the rates had dropped low enough even for his small purse. While sailing vessels had been built mainly to carry goods, steamships were constructed with passengers in mind. The steerage compartments of steamers were far from luxurious, but they were much more comfortable than equivalent quarters on sailing ships. For immigrants the real advantage of steamships was their speed, which cut an Atlantic crossing to ten days from the previous one- to three-months trips. Fast, cheap steamship service contributed to the increased flow of people out of Europe in the late nineteenth and early twentieth centuries. It also led to temporary migrations in which skilled German and British workers went to America in the spring and returned home in the fall. Quarrymen, miners, potters and textile workers made the seasonal trip to take advantage of America's high wages, but they had no intention of settling there. Steamship companies such as North German Lloyd and the Hamburg–Amerika Lines catered to immigrants, who were a great source of revenue. These lines did not have to advertise heavily because by that time Europeans had access to many other sources of information about America.

&2 "COME OVER AS I DID"

America had held a fascination for Europeans as far back as
Columbus' Day. But a shortage of first-hand information combined with widespread illiteracy in Europe gave rise to many
misconceptions about the New World. As late as 1827 a leading
German newspaper carried news from Texas and Virginia under
the heading "South America," and six years later an Irishman
asked for passage "to an Island called Upper Canada." The
Europeans' knowledge of life in America was equally distorted.
The romantic literature then in vogue pictured the New World
as a fairy-tale land filled with noble savages and earnest immigrants seeking the simple life. *The Leatherstocking Tales* by
James Fenimore Cooper was especially popular in Europe, where
it was read in every major language. People bored with their own
dreary lives thrilled to Cooper's dashing accounts of adventure in
the wilderness. While literature prompted people from every
European country to emigrate, it influenced none more than the
Germans. German children studied maps and travel books in
school while their parents pored over guidebooks, magazines and
travelogues in village reading clubs.

The Germans also led the parade of notable Europeans—
among them Charles Dickens—who made the Grand Tour of
America in the early nineteenth century. These visitors spoke
with the President, climbed the Allegheny Mountains, looked at
the serene rivers and bustling ports and wrote books about it all on
the trip home. Between 1815 and 1850 more than fifty such books
were published by Germans alone who had visited or emigrated

[83]

to America. Most of the European writers were favorably impressed with the United States and concluded that it was an extremely successful experiment in democracy. One of the most enthusiastic reporters was a wealthy German named Gottfried Duden, who lived on a Missouri farm for three years. Since he could afford to have someone else clear his land, Duden found pioneering to be great fun, and, in his abundant spare time, he wrote glowing passages about everyday farm life in America. Duden's articles were published as a book which became a best seller and the most important printed work in the history of German emigration. Peasants read his idylls with a growing longing to depart:

There are two varieties of deer here in Missouri, and they are for the most part very fat. The meat is savory, but the hunter seldom takes the whole animal with him. He is satisfied with the hind quarters and the skin, and hangs the rest of the animal on a tree so that some one else can take home a roast if he wishes.

· · ·

After breakfast I take my books in hand . . . I then busy myself as peacefully with the sciences as I ever did in Germany. Shortly before dinner I put them down and wander in the garden or to the spring and after dinner I go for a ride, either to visit the neighbors, or alone in the woods, on the heights, and in the valleys, delighting in the beauties of nature.

Unfortunately, most of those who took Duden's advice to emigrate to the United States did not have his financial resources and they found pioneering rough going in the beginning. Some disappointed settlers began to write criticisms of him and his highly romantic accounts of life in America. They called him Duden "Der Lugenhund"— Duden, the lying dog.

In quite another way the Federal Government was indirectly responsible for luring many immigrants to America. Under the Homestead Act of 1862, any citizen or alien who intended to become a citizen could receive one hundred and sixty acres by living on the land for five years and paying a small fee. Many people who barely eked out a living on five-, ten-, and twenty-acre plots in Germany and other parts of Europe immigrated to take advantage of this generous offer. Some Germans immigrated just to enlist in the Union Army, which entitled them to a land bounty at the end of their service. After the Civil War almost every northwestern state and territory from Wisconsin to the Pacific Ocean worked vigorously to attract settlers in hopes of spurring economic growth. Their immigration bureaus advertised widely in European papers, distributed thousands of pamphlets and maps on the Continent, and sent agents across the Atlantic.

Many American railroad companies were even more ardent in their pursuit of foreign settlers. They had been given vast tracts of land by the Government for building lines to the West, and they needed settlers to make their land—and their railroads —profitable. The companies were not thinking so much of immediate immigrant fares as they were of future income from hauling the farmers' produce east and bringing manufactured goods back west. The railroads spent large sums of money on their advertising campaigns in Europe and at one point the Northern Pacific employed eight hundred agents to attract immigrants to its forty million acres. Agents offered free "land-exploring" tickets, reduced steamship and railroad fares from Europe, easy sales policies, and long-term loans. Many of the lines built houses for immigrants where they could stay, free of charge, while they investigated property. The Great Northern Railroad taught settlers about pioneering on the plains and a few companies even built churches and schools for the communities they sponsored.

But the effect of all these incentives on prospective immigrants was nothing compared to the appearance of a visiting expatriate. Germans who had stayed home could not get over the emigrant's lightning fast change from penniless servant to substantial landowner. Or perhaps he had risen from poor apprentice to master of a hundred workers. This visitor was "living proof" of America's benign atmosphere and after contact with him others made haste to be off, too. Next to the returnees themselves, the letters they sent from America were the most convincing advertisements for the New World. The arrival of an "America letter" was a grand occasion and the whole village turned out to hear it read aloud. The letter-writers took their task seriously, for the postage cost them a day's wages. The letters were full of job information, general advice—and often large banknotes and prepaid passages. Lack of class distinctions and freedom to advance in America were frequently sounded themes in these letters. One man noted that a farm keeping eight horses was only taxed twelve dollars in America and another commented on the absence of beggars along the highways. Although the writers painted drawbacks as well as advantages to the move, none expressed the desire to go back to Germany. In the early 1830's one German-American farmer sent this typical letter home:

If you wish to see our whole family living in . . . a country where freedom of speech obtains, where no spies are eavesdropping, where no simpletons criticize your every word and seek to detect a venom that might endanger the life of the state, the church and the home, in short if you wish to be really happy and independent, then come here.

GERMANY IN AMERICA

The German immigrants got off to an auspicious start in America. Unlike the Irish and some other groups, they migrated in family units and put down new roots quickly and deeply. Being together in the New World seemed to lend them strength for they often overcame hardships that crushed unattached individuals. The Germans' path was also smoothed by the cash they brought from the sale of land or equipment in Europe. This money saved them from the initial period of suffering faced by so many penniless Irishmen arriving at the same time.

In the beginning some Germans went right to the frontier, but most came back to established settlements. Guidebooks, letters and rumors spread their advice: "Let Americans start a frontier clearing. Only they have the skills to do it." Later on, German immigrants usually bought crude farms from native pioneers who were eager to go farther west. Then the newcomers patiently settled down to expand and improve the property. Their hard work brought them prosperity and word of that prosperity drew thousands of Germans after them.

Some people in Germany were distressed to see so many of their countrymen go off to America. Would Germans in America forget all the old ways in their zeal to become "Yankees"? These people decided to channel emigration into organized groups that would preserve the old culture in the New World. Paul Follen, a leader of the Giessen Society, stated that his group might "in at least one of the American territories, create a state that is German from its foundations up . . . which may develop to be the model state for the whole commonwealth of man."

Starting in the early 1830's members of the Giessen Society and other organizations emigrated to New Orleans, transferred to steamboats for the trip up the Mississippi River and then fanned out along the Missouri River looking for fertile land. Their activities brought many Germans to Missouri and southern Illinois and at least one of their towns, Belleville, Illinois, became so thoroughly Germanic that many local inhabitants learned the immigrants' language. The Giessen Society had chosen its settlers on the basis of idealism and education, not farming technique. Consequently few of them knew how to go about establishing a rural home in America. Their neighbors called them "Latin farmers" or, less kindly, "educated fools." As one man described a visit to a typical "Latin farmer's" home in another area:

You are welcomed by a figure in a blue flannel shirt and pendant beard, quoting Tacitus, having in one hand a long pipe, in the other a butcher's knife; Madonnas upon log walls; coffee in tin cups upon Dresden saucers; barrels for seats; to hear a Beethoven's symphony on the grand piano; "My wife made these pantaloons, and my stockings grew in the field yonder"; a fowling-piece that cost $300, and a saddle that cost $5; a book case half-filled with classics, half with sweet potatoes.

The few practical farmers among them did well, but many of the others found their task hopeless. Some went to St. Louis, then a small frontier city, and tried to make their livings as doctors, lawyers, astronomers and mathematicians. Some committed suicide and others died as street beggars.

Undaunted by the failure of the Latin farmers, the colonization societies next directed their efforts toward Texas, which became an independent republic in 1836. At that time Texas was small enough to be greatly influenced—even taken over—by a large number of Germans. Interest in colonizing it grew until a traveler to Germany in 1844 found Texas the main topic of conversation among poor mountain people. In that year the *Mainzer Adelsverein* sent a group to Texas under Baron von Solms-Braunfels amidst much fanfare. But the group ran into difficulties from the start. Upon arrival they discovered that their land claim had run out and they would have trouble renewing it. The entire summer and fall slipped by while legal negotiations were under way. When seven hundred colonists came to join the original band no housing had been prepared for them and they had to camp out all winter. The following spring the colonists started their farms, but instead of the three hundred and twenty acres promised to them in Europe, they received only ten acres in the countryside and another half acre in the frontier town of New Braunfels. The settlers' disappointment over the land arrangements was matched by their discomfort from the heat, mosquitos and "frontier fevers." Baron von Solms-Braunfels proved such an inefficient manager that the colony's assets dwindled to nothing and the emigration company finally collapsed into bankruptcy. Some of the colonists went back to Germany, others enlisted in the Mexican War, and the majority scattered all over the United States. The efforts to colonize Texas did have some positive results, however, for by 1850, Germans accounted for 20 per cent of the state's population.

In addition to Missouri, southern Illinois and Texas, Wisconsin was vigorously promoted as the site of a "New Germany." In 1835 American supporters of colonization asked Congress for the establishment of several independent German republics here, mentioning the territory of Wisconsin as one possibility. Although Congress instantly rejected the proposal, the Germans hoped to gain control by sheer weight of numbers. Wisconsin appealed to the immigrants because of its rich, black soil and crisp air. In addition, many German Catholics were drawn to it because of the Church's activities in the area and the German bishop in Milwaukee. "New Germany" advocates had high hopes that an isolated settlement in Wisconsin would escape the "barbaric influences" that corrupted other colonies. Imbued with this idea, the *Arbeiter Bund* of New York sent settlers out from the eastern United States to form a colony in Wisconsin along communistic lines. However, the settlers dropped the communist ideology as soon as they started their own homesteads.

A desire to transplant the old culture was not the only reason Germans formed colonization societies. Some people started settlements for religious or charitable reasons, and others launched them simply to make money. While many of the people who came to the United States under a society's sponsorship did well as individuals, the projects themselves were doomed to failure. Self-imposed isolation ran counter to the pattern of American life and the colonies lacked a chief ingredient for success: individual initiative. Moreover, most German-Americans themselves opposed the ideas of "German nativists." The majority endorsed the philosophy of Carl Schurz, who wrote:

We as Germans are not called upon here to form a separate nationality but rather to contribute to the American nationality the strongest there is in us, and in place of our weakness to substitute the strength wherein our fellow-Americans excel us, and blend it with our wisdom. We should never forget that in the political life of this republic, we as Germans have no peculiar interests, but that the universal well-being is ours also.

SANGERFESTE AND TURNVEREINE

Whether the Germans traveled as part of an organized group or came alone, they brought many cultural gifts with them. One of the first items they "unpacked" was their love of music. Indeed, some of the immigrants even organized choral groups aboard ship. Herman Melville, the American author, saw the Germans making ready for their voyage to America and he commented:

Every evening these countrymen of Luther and Melancthon gathered on the forecastle to sing and pray. And it was exalting to listen to their fine ringing anthems, reverberating among the crowded shipping, and rebounding from the lofty walls of the docks. Shut your eyes, and you would think you were in a cathedral.

As early as 1814 German-Americans started the Handel and
Haydn Society of Boston and they formed others like it as immigration increased. Many Germans also recreated their village
singing societies in the United States. During the day the immigrants worked as farmers, carpenters and housewives, but at
night they became baritones, tenors and first sopranos. The
choruses started out by singing for the community after church
and at Fourth of July picnics. As more and more glee clubs
formed in an area, friendly competitions called *sangerfeste* developed. Each year these musical conventions grew longer, larger
and fancier until special buildings had to be constructed to hold
the crowds. In 1894 some ten thousand singers came to New
York for a three-day competition that cost fifty thousand dollars,
a royal sum in those days. At first the choirs were completely
German, but later other Americans joined and the glee clubs
lost their ethnic affiliations.

Through the Germania Orchestra, later called the New
York Philharmonic, German immigrants also helped popularize
symphonic music in the United States. The Germania Orchestra
was begun by 23 Forty-eighters, refugees of the 1848 revolutions,
who had been musicians in Germany. The Orchestra was slow
to develop a following because few Americans had as yet acquired a taste for good music. For years people of German descent
formed the majority of its audience. By making many tours of
America, however, the Orchestra stimulated a desire among
natives to hear more fine music and in time many cities outside
of New York could boast their own symphonic orchestras—
usually under the direction of a former Germania member.

Physical education was another area in which Germans led the way. During the Napoleonic occupation, nationalists introduced calisthenics to Germany as part of a patriotic movement. The program of exercises became popular and immigrants brought it with them to the New World. The Germans practiced their skills in clubs called *Turnvereine,* which sponsored history lectures as well as physical education and military drills. By 1853 there were sixty of these societies in America. Just as the *Sangerfeste* grew more elaborate, the Turner get-togethers came to include many events. Marching and "turning" were more pleasant when accompanied by music, so bands became a feature of their exhibitions. Then parades, concerts, speeches, plays, and balls were added. The YMCA adopted the Turner program and helped popularize it in this country. Eventually the public schools picked it up, making athletics compulsory for every school-age child.

The German influence on American education extended beyond physical training. The immigrants took a great interest in their children's education, fighting hard for the introduction of the German language into school programs. They also enthusiastically advocated state support of education and vocational training on the high school and college level. Mrs. Carl Schurz, wife of the celebrated Forty-eighter, started the first kindergarten —"children's garden"—in Wisconsin in 1856. Seventeen years later St. Louis instituted the German play school on a city-wide basis and today the kindergarten, like physical training, is a standard part of the American public school system.

Finally, the Germans introduced a new attitude here toward Christmas. The immigrants believed that Christmas should be a day for attending church services and holding pleasant family gatherings. In their immigrant trunks they carried ornaments for decorating large evergreen trees and in their minds they carried the words to "Stille Nacht." By contrast, New England Puritans had not celebrated the day and for some time there had even been a law against it in Massachusetts. In the West and South before the Civil War, groups of rowdy, drunken men roamed the streets making noise and playing practical jokes. But over the years Americans copied the way German immigrants celebrated Christmas so that today a decorated evergreen is virtually a national symbol of the holiday and "Silent Night" is a seasonal anthem.

✒ FRICTION

By 1850 it was readily apparent to observers that German immigrants and American natives enjoyed very different ways of living. Most travelers agreed with the visiting European author who wrote that the Germans' singing, dancing and other leisure-time pursuits "distinguish them from the Anglo-American people, who, particularly in the West, have no other pleasure than 'business.' "

The difference between American and German life styles was particularly marked on Sundays when respectable Americans went to church, then remained at home in accordance with Puritan tradition. But respectable Germans arranged picnics, attended concerts and held card parties. After church an immigrant family

Immigrants often found that their customs and
traditions differed sharply from those of native
Americans. Here, a lively scene in a German
restaurant depicted by an artist not entirely sympathetic toward the proceedings.

might sit for hours in a restaurant garden drinking beer, eating sausages, singing and listening to the oom-pah-pah of a brass band. Natives were scandalized by this behavior and tried to put a stop to it many times. But the immigrants felt so strongly about their Continental sabbath that when authorities in Davenport and Chicago tried to prevent them from drinking beer on Sundays, many normally law-abiding people rioted.

Opposing attitudes toward farming caused more friction between immigrants and natives. In Europe, Germans had had to be scientific agriculturalists and thrifty managers in order to make a living from their small plots. But in America land was so plentiful that most natives made little effort at soil conservation. In comparison to the Germans' own conscientiousness, Yankees seemed wasteful and lazy. Moreover, the immigrants condemned the lightheartedness with which Americans traded or sold their farms. Most Europeans looked upon their family plots as holy places to be handed down from generation to generation, but Yankees were more interested in pushing on toward the Pacific than in building up an inheritance. As one German farmer wrote home from Missouri in 1835:

There is scarcely a farm that is not for sale, for the American farmer has no love for home, such as the German has. I am building a smoke-house, a kitchen, a milk-house over one of the excellent springs near our house, a stable for the horses and one for the cows. My American neighbors say that I am building a town.

Over the years American hostility toward the newcomers deepened. Prohibitionists criticized the group for its beer-drinking and slave holders opposed it on the abolition issue. Other natives disliked the Germans because their language and customs were strange and their religious beliefs—over half were Catholic or free thinkers—seemed "dangerous." Besides, some Americans said, there were too many of them: an influx of over two hundred thousand in 1854 alone. All these negative feelings coalesced in the Know-Nothing movement of the 1850's, when German immigrants suffered the same abuse as the Irish.

In part, the Forty-eighters brought the Know-Nothings' wrath down on the heads of their fellow immigrants. The refugee intellectuals terrified Americans by espousing such radical political doctrines as socialism, communism and anarchy. They shocked church-going people by advocating atheism and a variety of unorthodox religious beliefs. Not only did the Forty-eighters embrace the new Republican Party, but they went beyond it in calling for the immediate emancipation of all slaves. While most Germans joined the Forty-eighters in support of the Republican Party, the majority—who were even more conservative than natives—condemned the refugees on every other count.

After the Civil War hostility toward the Germans began to fade. Americans looked on with approval as the hard-working immigrants built prosperous farms and businesses or attained the position of master craftsmen. Natives also respected the newcomers for their traditionally law-abiding ways. By the twentieth century the Germans had earned a secure place in American life. But that very security lulled them into overestimating their strength. During World War I the Germans tried to influence American foreign policy—with tragic consequences.

German-Americans maintained close familial, organizational and emotional ties to the Old Country. The expatriates carefully followed events in Europe, noting with pride their country's growing strength. When war broke out in Europe in August 1914, German-Americans rallied to keep the United States out of the conflict. The following winter they mounted a campaign to stop the Government from sending arms to the Allies. Americans became alarmed at the Germans' activities and their attitude toward the newcomers shifted from one of approval to one of suspicion.

As America mobilized for war, pressure mounted for conformity and a new kind of all-embracing loyalty to the nation. President Wilson led the campaign against foreign influences by attacking Americans who "need hyphens in their names because only part of them has come over," and Theodore Roosevelt called for an "America for Americans." In this emotionally charged atmosphere nothing less than 100 per cent Americanism became acceptable. The spirit of the times was clearly expressed when President Wilson called on Congress to declare war in April 1917: almost every person in the audience was wearing or holding an American flag.

America's entry into the war came as a terrible shock to German-Americans. Overnight they had to decide whether they were German or American, for they could no longer be both. Almost all Germans decided in favor of the United States: the boys marched off to war, the men bought war bonds and the women rolled bandages. But no good deeds on their part could convince inflamed Americans that they were not secret agents of the Kaiser. Indeed, some "patriots" even accused German-American Red Cross volunteers of putting ground glass in bandages and food destined for American servicemen. On several occasions mobs beat people of German descent and smashed store windows bearing German names. In many places German-American newspapers were banned, the study of the German language dropped from schools and German music omitted from concert and opera programs. Operating on the assumption that America would not be safe until the last vestige of the "Hun's" influence was wiped out, Americans went to the ridiculous extreme of renaming hamburgers "Salisbury steak" and sauerkraut "liberty cabbage." The Government lent its support to this hysterical campaign by giving semiofficial status to secret patriotic organizations, such as the American Protective League. The F.B.I. and the War Department gave these organizations leads on suspected subversive people and then their members went out to substantiate the accusations. In fact, the "evidence" they turned up generally consisted of gossip.

Shortly after the war, Americans regained their sanity and restored Germans to their rightful place in society. But all those of German descent who had lived through this harrowing experience would never again feel completely secure in America. As a community, German America never emerged from the war at all. Under great outside pressure most German singing societies, gymnastic associations and other voluntary groups disbanded. The German press, which at the outbreak of World War I had boasted more newspapers than all other immigrant publications combined, shrank to a fraction of its former size and influence. Reluctant to identify with the group after the war's debacle, scores of Germans anglicized their names and thousands more broke all ties with the group. With a few notable exceptions, the German-American simply disappeared.

GERMAN JEWS

Jews historically suffered widespread discrimination in Germany. They enjoyed a brief respite in the eighteenth century, but after the Napoleonic Wars ended in 1815, they once again found themselves the object of official intolerance. Several German states banished Jews from their territories. Other provinces and cities, such as Frankfurt, restricted them to crowded ghettos and regulated their communities down to the number of marriages they could contract each year. In Bavaria, where some villages were inhabited solely by Jews, the government imposed licenses upon those who wanted to practice a profession or engage in certain businesses. Since the number of these licenses was limited, young people saw little chance of obtaining them and they emigrated. By 1839, fifteen thousand Jews had left Germany, two-thirds of them from Bavaria. Their number continued to increase, but later emigration was caused less by religious persecution than by the prevailing economic depression that hurt Jew and Christian alike.

Most of the Jews who emigrated from Germany were tradespeople and professionals and they took up their work in cities and towns across America. A few of the immigrants had enough capital to set up stores immediately, but many had to put packs on their backs and trudge long miles to sell a spool of thread or a nickel-bag of sugar. These peddlers lived frugally in order to save enough money to set up their own stores. A few of the German-Jewish newcomers became extremely prosperous, especially those who went into banking, and they became members of America's most exclusive social and financial circles. Their co-religionists referred to them admiringly as the "Jewish Grand Dukes."

German Jews, "dukes" and lesser nobility were eager to fit into American life, and they even adapted their religion to suit the new country. In 1875 Rabbi Isaac Mayer Wise established a Reform congregation in Cincinnati in an attempt to Americanize Judaism. Rabbi Wise thought that American life moved too swiftly for Jews to practice the many rituals Orthodoxy demanded of them. According to the German Reform movement he imported, Jews worshipped on Sunday instead of Saturday and they used English rather than Hebrew in their services. They also dropped the traditional dietary laws. Later, members of Reform temples went back to Saturday worship and a third branch of Judaism, the Conservative movement, reinstituted other Orthodox practices. But many American Jews of all national backgrounds still worship in the Reform manner introduced by German immigrants.

When they sailed from Germany Jews shared their steerage quarters with Christians, and friendships that would have been impossible in Europe were forged aboard ship. Upon their arrival in the United States the Jews sought out German communities, where they mingled as equals. Jews frequented the same beer halls as other German-Americans and were accepted without bias into their pioneering societies and social clubs. Intermarriage between the two groups was fairly common. Then, with the onset of American anti-Semitism in 1881, German Jews began to identify less with their fellow countrymen and more with the Russian and Eastern European Jews who had started to enter the United States in large numbers. World War I further widened the gap because the Jews did not share their countrymen's pride in Germany's growing military strength. Later, the rise of Hitler made the break complete.

After assuming power Adolf Hitler wasted no time in starting his systematic persecution of Jews and intellectuals. From 1933 to 1941 he drove over one hundred thousand Germans and Austrians—about 80 per cent of them Jewish—to America. Among them were twelve Nobel Prize winners and hundreds of people of equal caliber. The refugees were atypical immigrants in that most were city-dwellers, and a large number were well-educated or skilled laborers. The hardships they faced were also unusual because many had endured grueling internment in concentration camps and heartbreaking family losses before reaching America. They arrived during the depths of the Depression—when even natives were having trouble getting jobs—whereas other immigrants had always come in flush times. Moreover, while manual labor is easily transferable, the German professionals had to learn English well and acquire licenses before being able to set up practice in the United States.

For most immigrants a factory job was a big step up in life, but for many refugees from Nazi Germany it was just the opposite. Nevertheless, the great majority put pride aside and accepted any job that could be found. It was not unusual for college professors to sweep floors and eye surgeons to wash dishes until they became reestablished in their own fields. With the aid of hundreds of generous American agencies and individuals this was soon accomplished and most refugees quickly adjusted to American life. In fact, they adopted the outward trappings of citizenship—language skills, naturalization papers, home ownership and American friends—faster than any other immigrant group. Their inward acceptance of the new country was equally swift and dramatic. What Thomas Mann, the noted German author, wrote of a fellow refugee applied to many:

This man is no emigrant who waits for the return to his Homeland. He does not look back. He is here, for good and with all his heart. America has gained him completely, and . . . many will feel that he is a gain for America.

The availability of free or cheap land drew
thousands of natives and immigrants to the frontier.
But the hardships of pioneering proved overwhelming for many settlers who soon returned to
established communities. DENVER PUBLIC LIBRARY
WESTERN COLLECTION

Vikings of the Great Plains

U PON ASSUMING THE PRESIDENCY IN 1865, Andrew Johnson predicted that it would take 600 years to develop America's vast western lands. But pioneers "closed" the frontier in 1890, cutting short the President's estimate by 575 years. Government incentives, railroad construction and new equipment each played an important role in the country's expansion. Another key factor was the influx of new immigrants—Norwegians, Swedes and Danes—who established thousands of productive farms in the Middle and Far West. These newcomers had been happy to exchange the rocky slopes of Scandinavia for America's fertile plains.

Today Scandinavia is highly industrialized and most people earn a good living in factories and small businesses. But in the nineteenth century the majority had to depend on the land and they perpetually suffered hard times. An extremely short growing season, mountainous topography and infertile soil plagued farmers. So much of the land was either heavily forested or otherwise unsuitable for crops that in 1850 only 4 per cent of Norway and Sweden were under cultivation. Since Denmark is endowed with larger expanses of flat land and somewhat milder temperatures, it enjoyed greater prosperity. This explains, in part, why fewer Danes emigrated. In all three countries noblemen and wealthy squires held much of the land and they did not sell it to the lower classes. Norwegian renters, while legally free, had to perform a multitude of services for their landlords, and those farmers who owned their land outright got so little return from it that independence was meaningless. To Scandinavians land meant freedom, citizenship and social status. But land was something one could only dream about in the Old Country. Completely thwarted at home, many people decided to emigrate when they read that in America land "is sold for $1.25 an acre. . . . Whether native born or foreign, one is free to do with it whatever one pleases."

The Scandinavians' plight became increasingly acute as the nineteenth century progressed. Improved sanitation, better medical treatment and wider potato culture brought down the death rate and caused the population to more than double. Large families became the rule. Except for the eldest son, who inherited his father's property, the children had reason to be pessimistic about their future. Many became hired farm hands, and in 1833 a Swede warned that his country was "in danger of acquiring what has never before appeared [here] . . . an agrarian proletariat."

In the second half of the nineteenth century many Scandinavians, from lumberjacks to carpenters, lost their jobs when iron replaced wood in the construction of ships. At the same time those young people who tried to advance themselves as artisans found their progress hampered by many old-fashioned guild restrictions. Along with other workmen, they suffered frequent periods of unemployment and chronically low wages. Tales of steady jobs paying up to seven times the average Scandinavian's salary lured many workers across the sea. Young women departed when they learned from "America letters" that in the New World "people are constantly looking for Norwegian and Swedish servant girls."

Economic opportunity was America's main attraction for Scandinavians—as it was for almost all immigrants. But many Norwegians, Swedes and Danes also emigrated to enjoy this country's tolerant religious atmosphere. Throughout Scandinavia the Lutheran Church operated as an official arm of government. Every citizen was born into it, was subject to its jurisdiction and had to support it with tax money. But many parishioners felt that the church had lost touch with the common people. They criticized the clergy for coldness, preoccupation with worldly matters and hard drinking. Convinced that Lutheran services had become mere formalities, some Scandinavians sought out a more personal religious experience in the missionary churches operating secretly in their countries. In time, Baptists, Methodists, Quakers and Mormons made many Scandinavian converts, and unordained ministers of various convictions, some quite exotic, attracted local followings. The Lutheran Church reacted harshly to this challenge to its authority, going so far as to jail dissenters. Its highhanded methods antagonized converts and staunch Lutherans alike. They responded enthusiastically to reports that in America "everyone can believe as he wishes and worship God in the manner in which he believes to be right, but he must not persecute anyone for holding another faith."

The strict class distinctions that divided Scandinavian society galled people even more than ecclesiastical tyranny. Under their countries' rigid caste system, men found it virtually impossible to rise above the station to which they had been born. Each class was jealous of its prerogatives and the free landholders were as overbearing toward the renters as the aristocrats were to them. On a visit home, one Swedish-American noted that, despite his success in the United States, to the aristocracy his "plain name and humble ancestry were . . . a fault that could never be forgiven." By contrast, a newly arrived Norwegian expressed the belief that in the United States "the principle of equality has been universally accepted and adopted. The artisan, the farmer, and the laborer enjoy the same degree of respect as the merchant and the official."

"OLEANA"

Unlike Ireland and Germany, Scandinavia did not do enough business with the New World to encourage an early, large-scale migration. After a flurry of interest in New Sweden in the seventeenth century, almost no Scandinavians moved to America for two hundred years. Then, in 1825, the "Norwegian Pilgrims"—a group of Quakers from Stavenger—settled in Rochester, New York. Their colony became a stopping-off point for fellow countrymen going west via the Erie Canal.

Just a handful of Norwegians followed the Stavenger Quakers to the United States until Ole Rynning led a group to Beaver Creek, Illinois, in 1836. During his second year in America, Rynning was severely frostbitten and he spent the winter writing his *True Account of America for the Information and Help of Peasant and Commoner*. This small guidebook created a sensation in Scandinavia, where it went through several printings in all three languages. So eager were Norwegian peasants to learn about the New World that many taught themselves to read by going over and over its pages. Throughout the book, Rynning tried to dispel myths and impart practical advice:

It is a general belief among the common people in Norway that America was well populated some years ago, and that a plague—almost like the black death—has left the country desolate of people. As a result they are of the opinion that those who emigrate to America will find cultivated farms, houses, clothes and furniture ready for them, everything in the condition in which it was left by the former owners. This is a false supposition.

. . .

People whom I do not advise to go to America are (1) *drunkards*, who will be detested, and will soon perish miserably; (2) those who can neither work nor have sufficient money to carry on business, for which purpose, however, an individual does not need more than four to five hundred dollars. Of the professional classes doctors and drug-gists are most likely to find employment; but I do not advise even such persons to go unless they understand at least how to use oxen, or have learned a trade, for example, that of a tailor.

Five years after Ole Rynning went to Beaver Creek, Gustavus Unonius established the first Swedish colony here since colonial times. His settlement at Pine Lake, Wisconsin, was short-lived, but it encouraged other Swedes to immigrate. The California gold rush of 1849 prompted Scandinavians of a different sort to try the New World. The young men who sought their fortunes in the gold field were adventurers, not typical immi-grants, and they did not establish any important colonies here. At about the same time, though, the Mormon Church initiated a program that had a permanent effect on the course of Scan-dinavian immigration.

When Utah became a state, the Mormons decided to sys-tematically encourage immigration to its colony in the Great Salt Lake Valley there. They sent missionaries to Europe and estab-lished the Perpetual Emigration Fund to help converts meet traveling expenses. Copenhagen was chosen as the Mormon's first base of operations in Scandinavia because the Swedish and Norwegian governments would not let them proselytize. Per-mission from the Danish government did not lead to total popu-lar approval, however. Outraged Lutherans, who did not consider Mormons proper Christians, pelted the missionaries with stones and smashed the windows of their homes. Undaunted, the Mormons continued to preach openly in Denmark and secretly in Sweden and Norway. Many people found the religion appealing and the promise of land in Utah enticing. In all about sixty thousand Scandinavians converted and half that number emigrated.

The Mormon converts' trek to Salt Lake is one of the most heroic chapters in American history. After crossing from the harbor to the Great Plains by train, the immigrants went to the Mormon's outfitting headquarters in Iowa City. Here they received supplies, which they loaded onto hand carts, and made ready for the thousand mile journey to Utah. Women and children walked alongside the men over scorching plains and wastelands. Some marchers tired of the exhausting hike and dropped out to settle in small villages along the way. But most Scandinavians finished the trip. They developed the colder areas of the Valley and ultimately, with other Mormons, created an oasis in the desert.

The Scandinavians' settlements at the Great Salt Lake prospered only through fine organization, almost superhuman energy and outside help. But most of their colonies, like those of the Germans, met a short and unhappy end. Oleana in Pennsylvania was one of their most publicized failures. Ole Bull, a famous violinist, put his life savings into Oleana, a 12,000-acre tract, which was to provide farms and jobs for poor Norwegians. There was much excitement in Norway over his Utopian plan and the common people hailed him as a great benefactor. Then, in 1853, the news leaked out that Bull had mismanaged the immigrants' affairs and had allowed himself to be swindled out of most of his property. The settlers' unhappy tales filtered back to Norway, where a newspaper editor seized on them to make fun of the exaggerated claims made for Oleana and America in general:

They give you land for nothing in jolly Oleana
And grain comes leaping from the ground in floods of golden manna.

The salmon they are playing, and leapin' in the brook, Sir.
They hop into your kettle, put the cover on, and cook, Sir.

The failure of Oleana did not discourage Scandinavians from moving to America. Rather, it confirmed their belief that they should go farther west. As the outflow of people from Scandinavia reached flood proportions, the emigration became a true folk movement and folk ballads grew up around it. The Norwegians adopted "Oleana" as their particular "marching" song because it reflected their high hopes for America and severed ties with a stingy homeland.

I'm coming, Oleana, I've left my native doorway.
I've made my choice, I've said good-bye to slavery in Norway.

✐ A TRUE FOLK MIGRATION

Before 1850 there were less than twenty thousand Scandinavians in America. Then, a series of poor harvests in Europe and the opening of new lands in the United States caused a sudden upsurge of interest in immigration. As early as 1851 a Norwegian newspaper commented, "In these days one continually meets the so-called Americans . . . who are on their way to the Norwegian colonies in the West." When the Civil War broke out, northern recruiters informed Scandinavians of the land bounties offered to soldiers who enlisted in the Union Army. So many men tried to take advantage of the Army's generous terms—and have their passage to America paid, besides—that the American consulate in Stockholm was soon beseiged by Swedes and Norwegians. "Furnish me with ships, or free passages," the consul wrote in 1863, "and I could take a quarter of the working population of this country to the United States next spring." But the Union could not spare any transports and the Civil War actually marked a short hiatus in the Scandinavian movement. When the War ended, immigration resumed on an even larger scale. The passage of the Homestead Act in 1862 drew thousands of Scandinavians to the Middle West, where they settled on the free government land. Many Swedes, suffering from a crop shortage so severe that it was known as "The Great Famine," fled to America to avoid starvation. Professionals, miners, sailors, and young men who wanted to avoid the draft all swelled the outgoing tide.

Through their letters the expatriates transmitted encouragement, advice—and prepaid tickets—to friends and relatives at home. Most of the reporters were pleased with their progress in the New World, often comparing America favorably with Scandinavia. "Generally our animals are larger here than they were in our home parish . . ." one newcomer wrote from Minnesota, "and the milk and cream are richer here than they were in Norway." Guidebooks and other travel literature also played their part in stimulating the desire to change countries. *Homes of the New World,* an informal work by the Swedish writer, Frederika Bremer, was particularly influential in directing Scandinavians toward the Northwest, which Miss Bremer described in glowing terms:

What a glorious new Scandinavia might not Minnesota become! Here the Swede would find his clear, romantic lakes, the plains of Skane, rich in grain, and the valleys of Norrland. Here the Norwegian would find his rapid rivers, his lofty mountains. The Danes might there pasture their flocks and herds and lay out their farms on richer and less misty coasts than those of Denmark.

Frederika Bremer's enthusiasm was highly contagious and by 1882, the peak year of emigration, "America fever" was raging through Scandinavia. It affected every province, every village and almost every family in Sweden and Norway. In some districts practically all the young people of the lower classes departed. In all, 1,250,000 Swedes, 850,000 Norwegians, and 350,000 Danes took up residence in America. While the Scandinavian movement seemed small compared to other groups, it was tremendous compared to the populations of Sweden and Norway—five million and two million respectively in 1900. Except for Ireland, no country lost a greater percentage of its people to America than Norway.

The mass exodus was viewed with great alarm in many quarters of Scandinavian society. Government leaders feared that emigration was sapping their countries of their most virile blood. The royal family of Sweden was so opposed to the movement that it offered crown lands on "better conditions than ever before" to keep people at home. Some ministers, eager to halt the flow from their shrinking parishes, read unfavorable reports of America from their pulpits, and most of them agreed with the clergyman who termed emigration a "feverish and diseased longing for greater earthly wealth." Aristocrats, too, condemned the movement to America, which it called the "paradise of rogues and rascals." The upper classes resented paying the higher wages that resulted from the wholesale emigration of workers and they felt threatened by America's equalitarian influences. Norwegians and Swedes both formed semi-official commissions to try to stem the outflow. As late as 1909 Sweden's anti-emigration society was exhorting its countrymen to "Listen to good advice! Stay in Sweden! Work and save!" But the westward impulse was not to be denied.

WESTERING

The Scandinavians' odyssey began with a trip to Hamburg or Liverpool, for few transatlantic ships called at Scandinavian ports. After debarking, usually in New York, the passengers continued their journey westward by whatever transportation was available. In the early years they had to travel long distances by ox-drawn covered wagons. Later, when the railroads added extensive feeder lines, they could ride in comfort almost all the way to their new property. New York newspapers carried accounts of Swedes marching from the harbor to the train in military formation, Swedish and American flags flying.

Often the immigrants received enough money from the sale of their European homes to take them as far as Chicago, Minneapolis, or one of the other Scandinavian-American centers. Here, they could board for a while with relatives while they became acclimated to American ways and earned enough money to buy their own farms. Some of the men took jobs as farm hands or lumberjacks, which they often had been in Scandinavia. Others found work connected with commerce on the Great Lakes or joined railroad construction crews. To aid the family fund married women took in washing and single girls hired out as domestics. After two or three years the immigrants usually had accumulated enough money to start a homestead or buy a semi-improved farm. One thousand dollars or more was needed in either case, for even when the land was free, the animals, equipment and special services required to start a farm were expensive.

Many immigrants would have preferred to settle down in an established community which could offer a Lutheran church and the comforts of civilization. But these amenities came too high for the average Scandinavian's purse. In 1848 a Norwegian visitor to Wisconsin noted the inflationary effect settlement had on prices:

It is said that the whole prairie is bought, except for a few undesirable parts, so that now one must pay considerably more than the government price. The price of wood has likewise increased so that it is far more expensive here than elsewhere to build houses and fences.

Throughout the nineteenth century newcomers sought out the frontier because land there was plentiful and cheap. In 1825 the Stavenger Quakers chose Rochester, New York, because it was the "Far West" of its day, and in the 1880's other Norwegians flocked to the Dakotas for the same reason. Unlike the Germans, many Scandinavians knew two or more homes in America. Their westering impulse became part of the larger American drive to reach the Pacific.

After the conclusion of the Sioux treaties in 1851, Scandinavians joined the caravan of pioneers streaming across the Mississippi. The settlers were so eager to take up the best lands that they did not even wait for the territory to be surveyed. In 1854 one pioneer woman wrote, "I believe the entire population of Wisconsin is on the way to the West now." Scandinavians poured into Minnesota, populating whole townships and putting four hundred Scandinavian names on the state map. From there, many moved on to Dakota and beyond: to Montana, Idaho, and the states of Washington and California. In the early 1900's, after the American frontier had been populated, a number of Scandinavians turned their sights toward Canada's vast western plains. But most remained in the great triangle bounded by the upper Mississippi and Missouri Rivers.

Advice from older settlers, land agents and railroad companies guided the immigrants in their choice of a frontier home. Just as recent arrivals in America sent information about the New World back to the Old, so pioneers reported their impressions of the frontier to friends in established communities. These letters were often published in the Scandinavian-American press and the Norwegian-language paper, *Emigranten,* featured one in almost every issue. When sending back an "America letter" from the frontier, a settler usually extolled the virtues of his particular area and urged others to move there. But as visitors sometimes found out, pioneers were not above exaggerating their success. A traveler to Wisconsin in the 1840's commented:

Their home was much poorer than any charcoal hut in Sweden, without floor, almost without roof, and with a few stones in a corner which were supposed to be a stove. Such was the magnificent house which they had written they were building to receive all the Swedes who would come. . . .

Frontier land often turned out to be as deceptive as the pioneers' reports. Before it was properly drained, much new territory was marshy, but it did not always give that impression. In a typical instance, Ole Rynning's men examined the land around Beaver Creek in late summer and found it to be perfectly dry. The following spring, after a series of hard rains, the property turned into a swamp. Not only was the low, wet land impossible to farm, but it became a breeding ground for insects carrying malaria. The prevalence of swamps all along the frontier encouraged the spread of serious diseases, such as malaria and cholera, that ravaged settlement after settlement. Without the proper sanitary facilities, drugs or trained doctors, pioneers found it almost impossible to cure their illnesses and the mortality rate was high, especially for infants.

Sickness was just one of the unpleasant aspects of frontier life that was glossed over in popular treatments of pioneering. Scandinavians, like other Europeans, had thrilled to the exciting adventures of imaginary backwoodsmen in America. But those who tried pioneering on the Great Plains often found reality a far cry from fiction.

⊷ PRAIRIE LIFE

The first thing a newcomer did when he reached the frontier was to construct a dirt and grass hut against a sloping piece of land. The shelter was seldom more than twelve feet square, yet it

Building a home was the first order of business on the prairie. Most pioneer families constructed simple sod huts, like this dugout, which they banked against sloping land. NEBRASKA STATE HISTORICAL SOCIETY

served as living room, dining room, kitchen, and sleeping quarters for the whole family. Light came in through the front door and smoke escaped through a hole in the roof. Living so close to nature, the settler sometimes found gophers popping up through the floor or rattlesnakes falling in from the roof. These unexpected visitors were just one reason why everyone was glad to move into his next, more substantial home. By comparison with the sod hut, even a log cabin seemed palatial.

Once the pioneer completed his first dwelling, he started to break up the soil for cultivation. This was a difficult task on the prairie, where the tough, matted roots of the grass tore ordinary hoes to pieces. Those who could afford it paid experienced men two or three dollars an acre to do the job. When the land was prepared, the farmer set about sowing his fields with a suitable crop, usually a hardy variety of wheat. The immigrant had a particularly hard time with all this initial work since often he could not afford horses and had to work with the clumsy oxen which had carried him west. In addition to his field chores, the pioneer had to build a fence to surround his livestock and a barn to house them. He also had to sink a well since there were no springs and few streams on the Great Plains.

Even after he got his homestead into production, the prairie farmer was constantly on guard against the forces of nature. Ferocious tornadoes materialized out of nowhere, sending everyone running for his cellar. Prairie fires started easily because the coarse, dry grass shot into flames at the slightest spark. Without roads or streams to stop them, the fires often raged out of control for hours. In some years long droughts parched the land, and in others great hordes of locusts swarmed over the prairie, eating everything that grew.

Besides being at the mercy of a harsh environment, the immigrant farmer found himself trapped in an economic situation that was beyond his control. When he advanced from subsistence to commercial farming, his crop became an item of trade subject to every fluctuation of the market. A financial panic on Wall Street or a bumper crop in Russia could drastically cut his profits. Ironically, it was the farmer's very success that hurt him in the long run because he overproduced, causing the prices of farm commodities to fall steadily in the 1880's and 1890's.

An even greater burden to the pioneers than natural or economic disaster was the isolation they had to endure on the Great Plains. Settlers often compared the prairie to a vast, empty sea and their houses to tiny ships lost upon it. During the summer, at least, they were busy and outdoors most of the time. But during the long winters they were often idle and barricaded inside their homes for weeks at a time by fifteen-foot snow drifts. The constant struggle for survival coupled with the absence of social activities brought some people to the breaking point. Beret, the Norwegian heroine of O. E. Rolväag's classic work, *Giants in the Earth,* is the prototype of all immigrants who slipped from loneliness to insanity on the frontier. More pioneers—native and immigrant alike—reacted to the situation by drinking heavily. A missionary who visited Norwegian settlers in Dane County, Wisconsin, in 1850 reported that "it was offensive to come within the sphere poisoned by their breath."

The difficulties of frontier life eventually drove many people to abandon their homesteads. Disillusioned pioneers by the score returned to established rural communities and industrial centers to become wage earners. But thousands of Scandinavians remained on the frontier until they had tamed the wilderness. Swedes alone brought more American land under the plow than the total area of Sweden! Danes developed fine dairy farms and cooperative creameries in Iowa, Minnesota and Wisconsin. In addition to blazing new trails of settlement, Norwegians manned the halibut, salmon, and whaling ships of the Pacific. Immigrants from all three countries went into mining, shipbuilding, carpentry, furniture production, and masonry work. The newcomers also figured prominently in the lumber industry of the upper Great Lakes' "big woods." They cut down the logs that helped build and furnish a million western homes and they introduced conservation techniques that are still in use today.

Scandinavians played an important role in the burgeoning
industries of the northwest, particularly in fishing,
mining and lumbering. When their picture was taken,
these men were poling logs on the Rum River in
Minnesota. MINNESOTA HISTORICAL SOCIETY

✍ PER HAKANSON BECOMES PETER HAWKINSON

In many rural areas of the Middle West Scandinavians were the
original founders and the majority of the inhabitants. Because
of their pioneer status they were free to shape communities in
their own image, a privilege usually reserved for colonists. Where
Scandinavians did come into contact with native-born Americans, they received a friendly welcome. Americans respected the
newcomers for being pioneers and landowners and found their
religion, which was generally an orthodox form of Protestantism,
to be above suspicion. With so much in their favor, it is not
surprising that Scandinavians were accepted into American life
more quickly than any other immigrants except the English.

The Scandinavians' strong desire to become Americanized also hastened their assimilation. The newcomers wholeheartedly supported the public school system, which adults took advantage of as well as children. And many of them—like immigrants of every nationality—voluntarily anglicized their names. Over the years Lars became Louis, Birthe became Betsy and Esbjorn was changed to Osborn.

Unlike the Germans, who often sought to preserve their culture intact in the United States, the majority of Scandinavians felt almost no group identity. Indeed, the peasants who immigrated were hardly aware of a national culture to be preserved. A few Scandinavian ministers tried to hold their congregations together through the use of the mother tongue, but most promoted the adoption of English. In a typical statement, one Swedish clergyman referred to the German Lutherans' campaign to continue using German in church services as "the preaching of a language rather than a gospel."

Most immigrants would have found it impossible, in any case, to keep their European language pure in America, because their new experiences demanded the use of new words to describe them. There simply were no Scandinavian equivalents for "ice cream," "reaper," "miles," and "homestead." Thus immigrants who swore they spoke no English were actually incorporating the new language into their speech without realizing it. Referring to this phenomenon, one professor wrote: "The foreign language was like a girdled tree, and the words withered and dropped away." Interest in their ancestral tongues faded quickly among the American-born. When Luther College was founded in 1861 some 80 per cent of the instruction was in Norwegian. By 1921 only 8 per cent of the classes were held in that language. And today at the University of Minnesota, in the heart of the American-Scandinavian community, Scandinavian languages are among the smallest classes in the school.

A desire to appear respectable in the eyes of older Americans led Scandinavians to adopt increasingly puritanical attitudes. Immigrant Lutheran ministers, who went to the frontier as missionaries to a heathen land, took the lead in conforming to already existing standards. When citizens of Madison, Wisconsin, criticized a group of Norwegians for despoiling the Sabbath by picnicking, drinking and singing after church, Scandinavian clergymen sided with the natives. The ministers condemned these activities for bringing the church into disrepute and therefore weakening it. Whatever weakened the church in America had to be wrong they reasoned even if it was right in Norway. This spontaneous puritanism was reinforced by contact with American religious institutions and in time dancing, card playing, and theater-going all came under the ban. The New England atmosphere became so pervasive that in 1890 a visiting Norwegian novelist found immigrant ministers preaching "Boston morals" instead of theology.

Just as most Scandinavians upheld the conservative position in Lutheran affairs, the majority also leaned toward the right in political matters. With German immigrants, Scandinavians were among the first to support the fledgling Republican Party. They endorsed its anti-slavery position and naturally favored its free homestead policy. In their enthusiasm for the G.O.P., some Swedes even flew Republican banners from their church spires. Over the years the immigrants consistently voted for the Party's more conservative candidates. When the second generation came of age they rebelled against everything their parents stood for, including their conservative political philosophy. American-born Scandinavians helped elect Robert M. La Follette, Sr., under whose governorship Wisconsin adopted a mild form of state socialism, and they rallied behind the Northwest's revolutionary Farmer-Labor Party.

AMERICA IN SCANDINAVIA

To discuss Swedish emigration is the same as to discuss "Sweden": there is hardly a single political, social or economic problem in our own country which has not been conditioned directly or indirectly by the phenomenon of emigration.

As this Swedish writer indicates, the mass movement to the United States brought about far-reaching changes at home. Scandinavians underwent a period of soul-searching in which they re-evaluated every aspect of their society. Under such slogans as "Move America to Sweden," reformers openly exploited the emigration issue to spur social legislation. In Norway one leader urged laborers to depart en masse to force the government and private employers to recognize their worth.

Statesmen debated the exodus on many occasions. Some felt that if the dangers of emigration were more widely publicized, more people would stay home. Others contended that Scandinavia had to be made more attractive to its workers if she was truly going to stop the drain. One legislator said that Europeans had to find out "why America in industry and several

In 1948 the United States issued a postage stamp to commemorate the efforts of Swedish pioneers in pushing the frontier westward. COURTESY OF THE U.S. POST OFFICE

other areas can offer workers such favorable terms, and what the reason is for its superiority . . . which has brought it about that in much America has become the teacher of the Old World." Both Norwegians and Swedes undertook to study American life systematically and exhaustively, culling the best features for imitation in Scandinavia.

The Scandinavian countries also urged expatriates to return and apply to the Old World the skills and ideas they had learned in the United States. Between 1880 and 1920 about one hundred and sixty thousand Swedes and fifty thousand Norwegians did go back, taking up residence in rural parts of their homelands. Those who stayed in the United States remitted millions of dollars annually to relatives in Scandinavia. This money helped alleviate poverty, pay off mortgages, and improve farms.

Prodded by their research and the returnees' testimony, the Swedish and Norwegian governments both embarked on programs of land reclamation. Sweden even attempted to develop a frontier in Lapland to substitute for pioneering on the Great Plains. Officials found from their studies that the most persistent grievance among the lower classes was their inability to acquire homes in Scandinavia. To correct this situation the governments encouraged new construction and liberalized home financing. They also promoted a more equitable distribution of land, and by 1950 over 90 per cent of all Swedish farms were owned by their operators. As a result of their efforts to match America's allure, the Scandinavian countries brought about tax reforms and universal suffrage, extended free education, levelled class distinctions, and encouraged more tolerant religious attitudes. Eventually, they advanced so far that the United States studied *them* for pointers on social welfare programs!

A Swedish prime minister summed up immigration's impact on his country this way:

Thanks to the Swedish immigrant, America became a living reality in almost every Swedish home and a challenge even to those who stayed in the old country, spurring them to seek new opportunities and to utilize modern American technique in order to raise the standard of living.

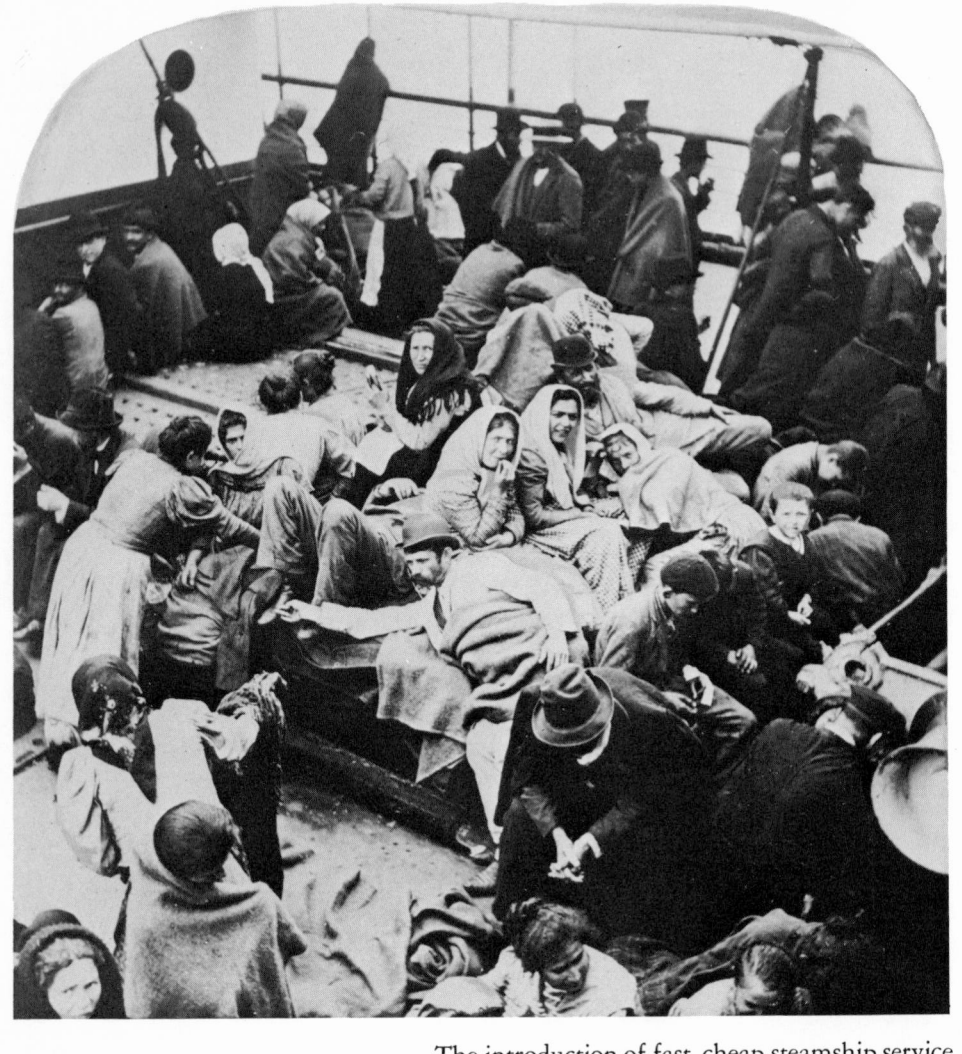

The introduction of fast, cheap steamship service
between southern and eastern Europe and the
United States was partially responsible for the sharp
rise in "new" immigration in the late nineteenth
century. LIBRARY OF CONGRESS

Of Floods . . .

AT THE END OF THE NINETEENTH
century northern and western Europeans, who had peopled
America since 1607, were showing less inclination to seek our
shores. By then the economic upheavals which had originally
pushed them from their homes had subsided and the frontier,
America's traditional attraction, was practically closed. Western
Europe's lower classes benefited greatly from industrialization.
Indeed, German factories came to employ so many men that
German farmers had to import agricultural workers from other
lands. At about the same time, too, western European governments discarded their laissez-faire attitude toward emigration.
Germany and the Scandinavian countries instituted reforms to
keep their citizens at home, and Great Britain, while not attempting to stop the outflow, successfully channeled it to her own
possessions and dominions.

These developments did not stop migration to the New World. Rather, they hastened a shift in the primary source of the movement, for just as the original stream began to taper off, a new influx from southern and eastern Europe was getting under way. By 1896 the "new" immigrants outnumbered the "old." But while the source of immigration changed, the basic reason people left home did not. Everywhere it was economic upheaval and worsening social or political conditions that caused the move.

✐ CHANGE

By mid-nineteenth century the breakup of feudalism, which had begun to take place in western Europe well over a hundred years earlier, reached the eastern portion of the continent. Then, within thirteen years of one another, the rulers of the Austro-Hungarian and Russian Empires freed all the serfs within their domains— a number far greater than the total population of the United States at the time. Emancipation brought immediate relief from feudal obligations, but it imposed other, more expensive, burdens. Where the peasants had enjoyed free access to the village wood-lands and meadows, now they had to pay for fencing, firewood and pasturing their animals. Where they had been able to barter, now they needed cash and cash was hard to come by. The men borrowed, bribed and took outside jobs to fend off the tax collec-tor or money-lender for another year. But after one or two crop failures they were often forced to surrender the land their families had worked for generations. Many former serfs became homeless wanderers, drifting from estate to estate. Others moved to the cities, where they manned new industries at very low wages.

Living conditions in eastern Europe in the late nineteenth century resembled Ireland's in the throes of famine. Home was a shack, crowded with children and older relatives and furnished with straw "beds" and a bench or two. To accommodate the fast-growing population, the land was divided and subdivided until twelve acres were considered an estate and plots smaller than five acres were common. With their unscientific farming methods the peasants could barely support their families on these tiny parcels. Their diet was a dreary round of bread, milk and potatoes and in some areas it was reduced to bread and water. Conditions grew so bad in Galicia, where many Jews lived, that several thousand people actually starved to death annually.

In addition to suffering these economic hardships, minority groups in Russia faced increasing persecution on political and religious grounds. They were the target of an official "Russification" program designed to stamp out the many different ethnic cultures within the Czar's realm. One of the first groups to be affected were Mennonites of German descent. In 1870 the government revoked the freedom of worship, draft exemption, and legal autonomy that they had enjoyed for decades in Russia. Later the government extended its program of harassment to include Russo-Germans of other religious persuasions as well. National policy towards Poles, who had openly rebelled in 1863, was especially repressive and eventually the Czar even curtailed the liberties of Finns, whose country enjoyed special status within the empire as an autonomous grand duchy. Russia's minorities seethed under the new restrictions and many emigrated rather than submit to them. Indeed, "aliens" constituted 95 per cent of the Russian exodus before World War I. Poles made up a quarter of the total and Russo-Germans, Finns and Lithuanians together accounted for another quarter. But by far the largest emigrating group—over 40 per cent—were Jews, who suffered the most drastic reprisals of all for being "different."

The assassination of Czar Alexander II in 1881 triggered widespread anti-Semitism in Russia. There were ever-harsher restrictions on Jewish religious, educational and professional activities and the government forced all Jews to reside within the Pale of Settlement, a crowded area on Russia's western borders. Barred from agriculture, the Jews could eke out only the barest of livings as artisans and peddlers. In some parts of the Pale ten Jewish peddlers competed for the business of one hundred peasants. In addition to facing economic hardships, the Jews lived in constant fear of being beaten, robbed and even killed by their gentile neighbors. Russian peasants vented their frustrations on the Jews and in several hideous massacres called pogroms, they slaughtered thousands of these helpless people. Jews met a similar fate in other parts of Eastern Europe, causing them to flee for their lives. Of the eight million immigrants from Russia and Austria-Hungary who settled in America, two and a half million were Jews.

Religious persecution was also behind the exodus from Syria and Armenia, two Christian islands in the midst of the Muslim Ottoman Empire. Discontented Syrians began to depart in the 1870's, while the Armenian movement got under way after the "Armenian massacres" of 1894–96. At first the Syrians took refuge in Egypt and India, but the influence of American

Protestant missionaries led later emigrants from both Syria and Armenia to set out for the United States.

The Greeks also suffered under Turkish rule, but they successfully revolted in the early nineteenth century. Independence, however, brought few rewards to the average person, who continued to face high prices, low wages and a worsening agricultural situation. Emigration from Sparta began in the 1880's, and spread throughout the country when the French market for currants, one of Greece's major exports, collapsed. With the establishment of direct steamship service between Piraeus and New York in 1902, "America fever" swept the country. So many men left home that only priests and the very old seemed to be left in some areas. By World War I one out of every four Greek men of working age was living in the United States. In all, three million people from Asia Minor and the Balkan countries made America their home.

Many Italians were as enthusiastic about the United States as the Greeks, for, if anything, they suffered even greater poverty. In the second half of the nineteenth century, southern Italy (which eventually supplied 80 per cent of the country's America-bound immigrants) simply could not support its burgeoning population. The land was worn out, scarred by wholesale deforestation, soil erosion and ancient farming methods. Moreover, absentee landlords owned much of the property and they were only interested in it as a source of quick profits. Tenant farmers and peasant owners were already in desperate straits when southern Italy lost two of its principal overseas markets. In the late 1880's, France imposed high tariffs against Italian wines, and the United States, once a large importer of oranges and lemons, developed its own citrus fruit industry. With the economy deteriorating rapidly, many Italians leaped at the opportunity to move to America. Population became Italy's major "export." By the turn of the century one Italian mayor was prompted to greet a distinguished visitor on behalf of his eight thousand constituents, "three thousand of whom are in America and the other five thousand preparing to follow them." To date more than five million Italians have settled in the United States, more than any other nationality except the Germans.

✑ THE GOLDEN DOOR

The extension of modern transportation into southern and eastern Europe in the late nineteenth and early twentieth centuries "greased the wheels of immigration." Trains picked up immigrants close to home and sped them to ports along the Mediterranean, Adriatic, and Baltic Seas, where steamships waited to take them directly to the United States. The steamship companies made a healthy profit on the "new" immigrants—even at thirty dollars a head for a steerage berth. Always eager to obtain more immigrant business, the companies distributed highly colored posters of the New World in coffee houses and other gathering places and sent agents throughout the countryside to peddle tickets. In Italy some of the more enterprising agents stationed themselves in front of churches to pass out printed hymns glorifying America!

The vast majority of "new" immigrants booked passage to New York. After a journey of ten to fifteen days they steamed slowly into New York harbor where they were greeted by one of the most spectacular views in the world. Skyscrapers of ten to twenty-five stories and, after the turn of the century, even forty stories, lined the Manhattan shore. To many immigrants who had never seen a building of more than five floors, the sight was particularly awesome. But even more thrilling was the Statue of Liberty, which dominated the harbor after its installation in 1886. The gigantic lady holding the torch of freedom seemed at once a goddess, a friend, and a symbol of the powerful country they were about to enter. The steerage was hushed as the immigrants, overcome with emotion, crowded to the rail to get a better look at her. No one who experienced that first encounter ever forgot it, and many years later the moment was still vivid.

When the ship landed the immigrants streamed down the gangplank, sometimes as many as fifteen hundred to two thousand strong. In the days before World War I, the bearded or mustachioed men were an exotic sight: Hungarians in rough jackets and high boots, Russians in furry Cossack hats and Rumanians in long sheepskin coats in every weather. The women, no matter what their country of origin, wore kerchiefs and shawls. As much a part of the immigrants' costumes as the clothes they wore were the bundles they carried and even the smallest children carried parcels scaled down to their size. In their knotted sheets and burlap bags the newcomers transported both practical items, such as teakettles, and sentimental objects, like framed photographs and bags of soil from the Old Country.

The government permitted immigrants in the two cabin classes to walk freely into America after only the briefest of shipboard interviews. But it made the newcomers in steerage undergo

Although immigrants traveling in first class were generally allowed to enter the United States after answering a few brief questions, steerage passengers had to undergo more extensive interviews and medical examinations before being admitted. LIBRARY OF CONGRESS

far more detailed medical examinations and personal interviews at Ellis Island. Preferential treatment of first and second class immigrants originated in the days of state supervision and the government carried over the custom when it assumed control of immigration in 1890. Although the practice was shockingly discriminatory and undemocratic, it was rarely challenged. Over sixteen million newcomers—overwhelmingly from southern and eastern Europe—submitted meekly to the system.

Immigration officials assigned numbered tags to the foreign steerage passengers and then ferried them to Ellis Island less than half a mile from the Statue of Liberty. Here the newcomers were processed in a huge room divided into a maze of pens and aisles. Terrified and confused, they lined up to meet the doctors. First, the immigrants were examined for signs of contagious diseases, mental incapacity, and physical handicaps that might impair their ability to earn a living. Next, they were given special eye examinations, for over half the medical deportations were due to trachoma, a contagious eye disease leading to blindness. Then, after waiting in the pens anywhere from a few minutes to well over an hour, the immigrants were interviewed with interpreters. The examining officers questioned them about their friends and relatives in America and their vocational plans in an effort to determine, in the words of the law, whether they were "likely to become a public charge." Upon completion of the interview, most immigrants received cards marked "Admitted" and they were ferried back to the mainland. Those who were not so fortunate could bring their cases before the review boards meeting in continuous session on the Island. About 5 per cent—from one thousand to ten thousand people a month—were rejected and sent back to Europe, but a few committed suicide rather than accept that fate.

While Ellis Island was sometimes the scene of tragedy, more often it was the site of happy events. Husbands and wives, parents and children who had been apart for months and years threw their arms around one another in joyful reunion. Hundreds of long-separated engaged couples, determined not to wait a moment longer, got married right at the reception center. Catholic priests were usually in attendance and judges or clergymen of other faiths were easily summoned to perform the ceremony. Ellis Island was also the meeting place for couples who were betrothed by mail without ever having met. Since the influx of "new" immigrants was overwhelmingly male at first, young men had little opportunity in America to meet and marry girls of their own nationality. They often solved that problem by writing home for a bride. While the prospective wife sent a photograph, the prospective husband did not and this was often disastrous!

With the ordeal of Ellis Island safely behind them, the immigrants dispersed. Slightly under a third stayed right in New York City, while the rest headed for industrial centers such as Chicago and Pittsburgh. Very few set out for rural communities. To be sure, many Czechs and Russo-Germans sowed wheat in North Dakota, some Poles grew onions and tobacco in Connecticut, and a number of Italians cultivated vegetables on truck farms across the nation. But they were atypical. For the vast majority of "new" immigrants America's siren song was not the wind whistling across open fields but the clack of hammers and the whir of machinery.

Italian immigrants at Ellis Island, 1905. Long
periods of waiting—for examinations, trains,
relatives—were in store for most "new" immigrants
after they landed in the United States.
GEORGE EASTMAN HOUSE COLLECTION

Between the Civil War and World War I, America's industrial output multiplied twelve times. In 1890, when agricultural production hit a record high and was still on the increase, manufactured goods surpassed farm commodities in value. As the twentieth century opened, the United States was the world's leading industrial nation.

Industrial expansion attracted "new" immigrants to America and their coming, in turn, greatly accelerated the pace of that growth. By 1910 the foreign-born, two-thirds of them from southern and eastern Europe, made up well over half of America's industrial labor force. Their names were especially prominent on the employment rolls of New England textile mills, Chicago slaughterhouses, New York clothing factories, and Pennsylvania coal mines and steel mills. Indeed, immigrants played such an indispensable role in America's economy that it is hard to believe they constituted only 14½ per cent of the population. The answer lies in the composition of the incoming throng: overwhelmingly male and overwhelmingly young.

Qualitatively as well as quantitatively, "new" immigrants profoundly influenced the course of industrialization. By providing a seemingly limitless supply of cheap, unskilled labor, the newcomers encouraged employers to do away with skilled labor, which was expensive and scarce. In place of skilled craftsmen, manufacturers installed machines which unskilled immigrants could easily operate. Mechanization together with immigrant labor brought down production costs, yet allowed buying power to grow.

The most recent immigrants always did America's
arduous and dangerous work, while those who
had come before advanced to better jobs. Here,
men erect supports in a Colorado mine.
DENVER PUBLIC LIBRARY WESTERN COLLECTION

When "new" immigrants entered a field, that industry often experienced a wholesale change of personnel. But far from robbing native and "old" immigrant employees of jobs, the newcomers actually accelerated their ascent into technical and executive positions. Thus, when Hungarians, Poles and Italians replaced German, British and Irish workers in the bituminous coal fields, the latter became foremen or sought better opportunities in the newer mines of the West. As an astute observer noted in the *North American Review* in 1892:

When the foreigner came in the native engineered the jobs, the former did the shoveling. The American in every walk and condition of life . . . has been the "boss" ever since. The foreigner plows and sows, the native reaps . . . one digs the canals, the other manages the boats; the one burrows in the mines, the other sells the product, and so on through all the various occupations.

Throughout American industry, long hours, low pay, and dangerous and unhealthy conditions were the rule and the "new" immigrant, on the botton of the economic ladder, got the worst of it. Captains of industry showed a singular lack of concern for their employee's welfare. They assembled and dismissed work crews at will or summarily fired an employee who had fallen ill. The men, largely unorganized into unions, had no way to collect sick pay, accident insurance or unemployment benefits—compensation we take for granted today. In some industries the pace of work was constantly being accelerated until the laborer found himself racing through his chores just to keep up.

Steel, like other heavy industries, employed thousands of "new" immigrants who often worked twelve-hour shifts, seven days a week under notoriously bad conditions. In 1919, when

British steel workers averaged forty-seven hours a week, their American counterparts were putting in sixty-eight. The following excerpt from a steel worker's diary graphically illustrates what the workers had to contend with:

You lift a large sack of coal to your shoulders, run toward the white hot steel in a one hundred-ton ladle, must get close enough without burning your face to hurl the sack, using every ounce of strength, into the ladle and run, as flames leap to roof and the heat blasts everything to the roof. Then you rush out to the ladle and madly shovel manganese into it, as hot a job as can be imagined.

Both natives and immigrants complained about the hazardous and exhausting nature of steel work, but the "new" immigrants were particularly bitter because they were consistently relegated to the dirtiest, heaviest and lowest-paying tasks in the mills. Even the second-generation men who were born in this country and who spoke unaccented English found their advancement blocked by native or "old" immigrant foremen. A Senate committee investigating the causes of the 1919 steel strike, in which three thousand men walked off their jobs in protest, heard bitter complaints of discrimination from the immigrants. The committee reported:

A Czech . . . feels that he is discriminated against because he is a hunky [derogatory term for an unskilled immigrant workman]. Several times when he has asked for promotion he has been told that the good jobs are not for hunkies. He feels that the clean, decent jobs are for Americans only.

Two Poles . . . feel they are exploited by the heater and roller who can rest at intervals while the remainder of the gang, foreigners, must work steadily and even snatch bites of lunch while working. Always when they ask for better jobs they are told to wait.

Immigrants could advance themselves somewhat more easily in the garment trades than in the steel industry, but the conditions under which they labored were equally abominable. The tenements of New York's Lower East Side were the scene of that vicious process of clothing manufacture, the "sweating system." It chiefly benefitted the manufacturer who, by contracting out most of his work, could evade responsibility for the conditions under which his garments were made. The subcontractor or "sweater" took home precut garments to be sewn by his six to fifteen "sweating" employees. His shop was generally one of the two rooms he rented in a dilapidated tenement house. Dark, airless, and crowded with the owner's belongings as well as those of the workers he boarded, the sweatshop was almost impossible to keep clean. In 1895 an investigator concluded; "A large proportion—nearly, if not quite one-half—of all the clothing worn by the majority of our people is thus made under conditions revolting to humanity and decency, and such as to endanger the health of the wearer."

In the garment trades, as in many other fields, the "new" immigrant often found himself being exploited by a member of his own ethnic group. Indeed, the few newcomers who became foremen or employers generally did so by climbing on the backs of their fellow countrymen. The labor boss or *padrone,* as the Greeks and Italians called him, served as employment agent, banker, and group leader. He rounded men up and sent them (sometimes as strikebreakers) where they were needed and over-

A New York sweatshop about 1890. For many
years, most American ready-to-wear clothing was
made in grimy tenement apartments such as this.
Photograph by Jacob A. Riis. THE JACOB A. RIIS
COLLECTION, MUSEUM OF THE CITY OF NEW YORK

saw their work. In the beginning, newcomers were often happy to place themselves in the boss's hands. Without his help in obtaining work, food and lodging they would have been at a complete loss. But as the immigrants became better acclimated to their new lives, they saw that the padrone was paying them peon wages and taking advantage of them in other ways and they left his service. As Dominick Ciolli related in his article, "The Wop in the Track Gang":

The money was all sent to the boss, who first took out of it whatever the men owed him for food. If a man [tried] to save more, buying little food, the *padrone* [charged] him a certain sum just the same. I kept a list of the boss's prices and the store prices at one city in Ohio, and always the boss's were 200 to 300 per cent higher. Sometimes the men would buy what they had to [from] the boss, throw it away, and go into the city to buy.

In their desire to get ahead, workers sometimes became their own hardest taskmasters. The temptation to overwork was especially great in the clothing, glove, artificial flower and cigar industries which paid by the piece rather than by the hour. To get done as many pieces of clothing as possible, sweat shop employees often ate at their machines and fell asleep on their material. In the tenements one heard "the whir of a thousand sewing machines worked at high pressure from earliest dawn till mind and muscle give out altogether."

The "new" immigrants often pushed themselves to the limit of human endurance because money represented to them what a homestead had to "old" immigrants: security, power, and prestige. They were not especially greedy or materialistic, but they had been completely at the mercy of their environment in Europe and it was important to them to be in control of their lives in America. On the Other Side, family, land or piety gave status to a peasant; in America, money talked. With it, the immigrant was "somebody" in his little world of the market, clothing store and café.

HOW THE OTHER HALF LIVED

Industrialization's companion was the rise of the city. In 1850, when the economy was largely agricultural, 87 per cent of the population lived in rural communities. But after the Civil War, when America's industrial machine shifted into high gear, natives —and immigrants—increasingly flocked to cities and industrial towns in search of jobs. By 1920 over half the population was urban.

What did American farm boys and European peasants find on their arrival in the city? Were they greeted by broad, tree-lined boulevards, glittering shops and gracious homes set on wide lawns? Could they rest awhile in grassy parks where fountains bubbled? Far from it! In the late nineteenth century American cities were uniformly crude, drab, filthy places which were bur-geoning without plan or concern for their inhabitants.

Urbanization created special problems that demanded new systems of organization. Garbage collection, sewage disposal and other necessities which had been simple matters in the country suddenly became major operations when expanded to cover city populations. But Americans, so inventive and progressive in other areas, were slow to attack these problems. Local governments took decades to install sewer systems and some municipalities used exposed drains until well into this century. They compiled an even poorer record when it came to providing recreational facilities. Except for New York, which set aside that wonder of urban America, Central Park, large cities gave almost no thought to establishing substitutes for the country's open green spaces. Indeed, Cleveland, Pittsburgh and Newark devoted more of their land to cemeteries than to parks. Nor did cities consider the special recreational needs of children until 1885, when Bostonians experimented with two heaps of sand and proclaimed them a "playground." But the worst feature of city life—and the one officials seemed most reluctant to control—was the overcrowding. In the second half of the nineteenth century the populations of New York, Chicago and other cities increased by 50 to 100 per cent every ten years, while new construction proceeded at a much slower rate.

With cities growing at such breakneck speed, land prices soared. To make the most of their expensive urban properties, landlords erected tenements—multiple dwellings which utilized every foot of space on a building plot. Tenements varied in design, but everywhere they were monotonous and unattractive row houses. In New York and Boston they were completely attached to their next-door neighbors except for a slight indentation on either side, dumbbell fashion. The six-story buildings were honeycombed with tiny rooms, hundreds of thousands of which were totally without fresh air or natural light. One young tenement dweller described her home as "a place so dark it seemed as if there weren't no more sky." Since the tenements were constructed in the shoddiest manner, their inhabitants had to endure stinking heat or numbing cold, depending on the season, and a complete lack of soundproofing. Moreover, all the tenants on a floor had to share one bathroom. With no garbage disposal facilities and no maintenance services to speak of, the tenements were destined to become slums.

Tenements "spread over Manhattan Island like a scab." In his classic study, *How the Other Half Lives,* Danish-born reformer Jacob Riis estimated that three-quarters of New York's working class lived in them in 1890. But not even these multiple dwellings could keep pace with the city's fast-growing population. The housing shortage grew so acute that thousands of poor people had to live in basements and subcellars, while others took up residence in former outhouses or hastily-built shacks behind the regular tenements. Although living quarters were not as crowded outside of New York, they were equally dilapidated and uncomfortable. Even in industrial towns, where land was relatively cheap, employees had to make do with rude cabins.

These "new" immigrants saw the very worst aspects of city life because they were poverty-stricken upon arrival and had only irregular and poorly-paid work for sometime thereafter. Since they could pay the least, they were forced to take the worst housing in the most congested and decayed parts of town. Back of the Yards, near Chicago's slaughter houses; the North End, in the midst of Boston's docks and markets; the Lower East Side, next to New York's East River traffic and "Little Italys" and "Little Polands" from coast to coast housed the most recent immigrants in filthy, hazardous conditions. As in industry, when the newest group came in the older arrivals advanced—in this case to better

Overcrowded, poorly maintained and lacking the
proper sanitary facilities, tenements inevitably
became slums. Yet for "new" immigrants, such as
the family pictured here, tenements were essential.
Photographed by Jacob A. Riis. THE JACOB A. RIIS
COLLECTION, MUSEUM OF THE CITY OF NEW YORK

neighborhoods with nicer homes. Indeed, by 1910 immigrants had the slums to themselves: a survey published that year could not cite a single tenement inhabited by native-born families.

In the end, immigrants paid dearly for their "cheap" housing. Epidemics spread rapidly through the dirty, airless tenements and tuberculosis ravaged whole neighborhoods. The most crowded sections, the ones where immigrants clustered, had the highest death rates, with infant mortality leading the list. Indeed, in one Chicago precinct at the end of the century, 60 per cent of the newborn babies born died in their first year.

For the "new" immigrants—former peasants—the transition from country to city was difficult. The women had to learn how to shop, keep an apartment clean and raise a family under the most trying new circumstances. The men had to adjust to earning a wage, traveling to work, and being dependent on others for a job. But the confinement of the city tenement was the most disorganizing element of all. Unaccustomed to such close living quarters, the newcomers became nervous and depressed. Housewives strung up sheets to create some privacy but there could be no privacy with as many as ten people, family and boarders, in two small rooms. Marriages broke under the strain and some immigrants were driven to alcohol, gambling and insanity.

GHETTO LIFE

Immigrants tended to live among their own kind in compact neighborhoods which were eventually called ghettos. Like all slum areas the ghettos were high in petty crime, broken homes, truancy, and misery. But they were also characterized by a warmth, color, and mutual concern absent in the more prosperous and anonymous parts of the city. New York's Lower East Side, home to some seven hundred thousand eastern European Jews in 1916, was the first place in America to be called a ghetto.

Since apartments were so crowded on the Lower East Side, they became little more than places to eat and sleep. All other activity moved out into the streets. Weather permitting, the Jewish immigrants slept on fire escapes, washed clothes on the roofs and chatted on the stoops. People hung out of every window in search of fresh air and a bit of diversion. As they looked down on the street, they saw vendors hawking every imaginable item from coal to second-hand blouses. Pushcarts lined the streets and merchandise crowded the sidewalks. The suspender man carried at least fifty pairs on his shoulders and many other salesmen were similarly their own display cases. There was no such thing as a fixed price on the Lower East Side. The final sale fell somewhere between what the seller dreamed of obtaining and what the buyer hoped to get away with. As the peddler and housewife argued over a price, their voices carried to the highest tenement window.

There were almost as many clubs on the Lower East Side as there were pushcarts and the legend LECTURE TONIGHT appeared on every second block. Indeed, self-improvement was practically an obsession in the ghetto, where immigrants flocked to art and English-language classes or joined political discussion groups. Through Yiddish, a dialectical German liberally sprinkled with Hebrew and English words, this generation of eastern European

Jews had become highly expressive. In fact, both the Yiddish press and theater set new standards of excellence. While every ethnic playhouse filled its seats by showing broad comedies and immigrant soap operas, theaters on the Lower East Side also presented plays with intellectual underpinnings. Yiddish drama was outstanding for its stark realism at a time when most American plays were still stiff, operatical works that bore no relation to real life.

Much of the Lower East Side's intellectual life revolved around the area's three hundred or so coffee houses, fixtures in every "new" immigrant enclave. Here, men sat far into the night sipping hot tea through sugar cubes and passionately arguing the merits of a political ideology or a theatrical performance. While the intellectuals were most concerned about events in Europe or the ghetto, they also took a passing interest in the American scene. Like the German Forty-eighters and other immigrant intellectuals, the Jews were usually critical of what they saw. In his amusing book, *Moscow-on-the-Hudson,* about fellow exiles from the Russian Revolution of 1917, M. K. Argus dryly describes a mentality akin to that of ghetto coffee house habitués:

The intellectual standards of Americans, we observed, was very low. . . . Who ever heard of a nation whose newspapers headlined ball players, printed on their front pages stories about mothers-in-law, and called their president "Cal," as if he were a dog! It was manifest that such people could have no real, serious literature; of this we were certain. America, we know, had produced a few good writers, but Russians were better acquainted with them than Americans. Whenever we met a native, we invariably asked him, had he read Bret Harte? (There is no *h* sound in the Russian language, and we pronounce it "Bret Garte.") He had not, of course. Had he read Jack London? Had he read Mark Twain's immortal story about the boy Gookelberry Finn? No American ever heard of Gookelberry Finn—a fact we used to point out triumphantly and venomously whenever we discussed the glaring shortcomings of American cultural life.

The Lower East Side had a religious life that matched its intellectual side in vigor. Judaism had been a way of life in Europe and older immigrants were determined to transplant it intact in the New World. Almost to a man they were Orthodox: the men praying three times a day and the women observing dietary laws in the home. On Friday afternoons the vendors put away their goods early and the normally overflowing streets were deserted. The Lower East Side stopped for Sabbath prayer. As their world expanded beyond the ghetto, many of the younger immigrants and second-generation Americans became impatient with the restrictions of Orthodoxy. They sampled American foods, not all of which were kosher, and began to attend the theater on Friday nights. Although many newcomers found Orthodoxy incompatible with American life, they were even less comfortable with the German Reform movement, which did not seem to be Judaism at all. Eventually, most of the younger immigrants and their offspring joined the Conservative branch of the religion which maintains modified Orthodox ritual.

Next door to the Jewish ghetto of lower Manhattan, Italian Catholic immigrants were also attempting to reconstruct the religious framework of their former lives. Once a year in Italy each village and region honored its patron saint with lavish ceremonies. The immigrants transported this practice to the New World, and in the warm months worshippers from Naples, Sicily, or Calabria could be seen marching in procession with ornate candles. Before they amassed enough money to build a proper chapel, the immigrants improvised temporary outdoor shrines which they covered with sheets. They adorned the shrines with jewelry and dollar bills, collections which sometimes netted as much as $20,000 for the church building fund. Certain holidays required that the worshippers do penance, and in the early years of Italian immigration it was not unusual for them to walk six miles or more barefoot on hot asphalt while saying their rosaries.

In conjunction with the religious ceremonies, Italian immigrants held great sidewalk *festas*. Colored lights were strung across the streets and every store and house was festooned with flags, flowers, and streamers for the occasion. Visitors strolled from booth to booth sampling the great variety of food and trying their hands at games of skill and chance. All too soon the *festa* ended with a glorious display of fireworks, music and dancing. Over the years the Italian street festivals lost their spontaneous folk quality and degenerated into mere commercial ventures. Those that survive today are pale imitations of the joyous saints days that meant so much to homesick immigrants.

There were so many unique and positive aspects to the ghetto that from afar we are tempted to romanticize it. But those who actually lived in the tenements were under no illusions about the quality of life there: they directed every energy toward escape. A father would put each member of the family to work, add still another boarder to the crowded apartment and deny himself all but the barest necessities. And when he had scraped together enough money, he would move his family out to a little better building in a slightly less crowded neighborhood. This mobility, so crucial to the immigrants' progress in America, was denied to Jews in Europe and is still denied to many ghetto-bound blacks in the United States today.

The eastern European Jews were helped out of the slums by their German co-religionists. Having blended successfully into American life, the German Jews did not care to associate with the "unassimilated" newcomers, but they did give them generous financial support. Settlement houses, social agencies of many kinds and free libraries gave the immigrants other kinds of assistance. But the most important single aid to their advancement was free public school education, which in New York City extended right through college. Taught by their parents that education was the key to success in American life, first and second generation children were sometimes more dedicated to their studies than other classmates were. In her autobiography, *The Promised Land,* Mary Antin relates what the gift of education meant to her, a Jewish girl who had been denied schooling in Russia because of her religion:

Education was free. That subject my father had written about repeatedly, as comprising his chief hope for us children, the essence of American opportunity, the treasure that no thief could touch, not even misfortune or poverty. It was the one thing that he was able to promise us when he sent for us: surer, safer than bread or shelter. On our second day I was thrilled with the realization of what this freedom of education meant. A little girl from across the alley came and offered to conduct us to school. My father was out, but we five between us had a few words of English by this time. We knew the word school. We understood. This child, who had never seen us till yesterday, who could not pronounce our names, who was not much better dressed than we, was able to offer us the freedom of the schools of Boston! No applications made, no questions asked, no examinations, rulings,

exclusions; no machinations, no fees. The doors stood open for every
one of us. The smallest child could show us the way.

As the humorist Harry Golden recalled years later, "On
the Lower East Side in the early years of this century we came
as close to any guarantee as life has ever offered. The guarantee
was if you worked hard, went to school, studied and saved, you
could participate in America." But many Jewish immigrants and
their offspring found that there were distinct limits to this participation. Americans, alarmed at the meteoric rise of the Jews,
began to erect barriers against them in every sphere of activity.
Natives also discriminated against other "new" immigrants as a
wave of xenophobia swept the United States in the early twentieth century.

... *And Dams*

AFTER THE TURN OF THE CENTURY
"new" immigrants debarked at an unprecedented rate. They regularly surpassed the "old" immigrants' peak year record of 788,000 arrivals and in 1907 they set their own record of 1,285,000 that will probably stand for all time. Noting this tremendous influx, natives became fearful that they would be engulfed by foreigners. Americans forgot their own antecedents and wondered how the "new" immigrants—so alien in appearance and custom—could be assimilated. For the first time the American people as a whole seriously questioned the wisdom of admitting all comers. Yet up to this point they had endorsed a laissez-faire policy of immigration, even if, at times, they seemed to fear the consequences of that policy.

By the turn of the century immigrants from southern
and eastern Europe were passing through Ellis Island at
a startling rate. In 1907, 1,285,000 newcomers were
admitted to the country, a record that will probably
never be equalled. LIBRARY OF CONGRESS

✎ WELCOME

Ever since colonial days Americans had been dedicated to the principle of growth through immigration. In the Declaration of Independence they accused King George III of having "endeavored to prevent the population of these States; for that purpose obstructing the Laws for Naturalization of Foreigners; refusing to pass others to encourage their migration hither, and raising the conditions of new Appropriations of Lands." As soon as independence was won, George Washington made America's offer of asylum official. In 1783 he declared, "The bosom of America is open to receive not only the opulent and respectable stranger, but the oppressed and persecuted of all Nations and Religions." Yet only fifteen years later, when war with France threatened, Congress hastened to protect the country from the foreigners in its midst with the Naturalization and Alien Acts. These laws extended the residency requirement for citizenship from five to fourteen years and empowered the President to deport any alien he deemed a threat to national security. Once the war scare passed, however, Americans recoiled from the harshness of the Acts, restoring the original residency requirement and allowing the Alien Acts to lapse without renewal.

While there were no other major incidents of nativism in the early years of the Republic, some people did express anti-foreign sentiments. They were afraid that unrestricted immigration would swamp the country with Europe's excess population and all its attendant social ills. In 1797 a member of Congress argued that immigration had been beneficial when the country was new and unsettled, but now that America was mature and fully populated, the movement should be terminated. In 1836 a New Yorker, observing the crowds of newcomers thronging the port, voiced another complaint of nativists from the eighteenth to the twentieth centuries:

All Europe is coming across the ocean, all that part at least who cannot make a living at home; and what shall we do with them? They increase our taxes, eat our bread, and encumber our streets, and not one in twenty is competent to keep himself.

Since the shortage in America was of men, not acres, it was in the nation's best interest to encourage immigration and the Government continued to extend a generous welcome to foreigners. In a message to Congress in 1841 President John Tyler reaffirmed Washington's earlier greeting. He stated, "We hold out to the people of other countries an invitation to come and settle among us as members of our rapidly growing family. . . ." But as slavery, sectionalism, prohibition and other issues threatened to tear the country apart in the 1850's, many Americans blamed Irish and German newcomers for creating national tensions and thwarting personal goals. In general, nativists sought to restrict immigration. In particular, they wanted to curb the growth of the Catholic Church, which had been an object of suspicion to Protestant Americans since colonial times. At one point the nativist Know-Nothing Party demonstrated great strength at the polls, only to lose support quickly when the Civil War became imminent. But anti-Catholicism remained below the surface to emerge at other times of national upheaval.

During the Civil War President Lincoln called for a "system for the encouragement of immigration" and a bill to that effect was passed by Congress in 1864. Although the law was never acted upon, the Federal Government continued to speak favorably of immigration, usually citing its economic value. The Treasury Department issued a statement estimating that each immigrant was worth $800 in the national coffers. In the decades following the Civil War other official spokesmen substantially raised that figure. Although its liberal land policies induced many Europeans to move to America, the Federal Government did nothing to directly encourage immigration. The western states and territories, on the other hand, launched vigorous and successful campaigns to recruit settlers from abroad. During Reconstruction, the southern states, too, formed elaborate committees to attract foreign labor, but few immigrants were ever attracted to that section of limited opportunity.

The immigration laws of the states and ports handling incoming passengers carried out the spirit of America's indiscriminate welcome. These laws sought only to bar those who would be a permanent drain upon society, such as the insane, but they in no way attempted to inhibit the entrance of normal persons. When the Federal Government assumed control of immigration in 1882, it merely codified the existing state laws and did not go beyond them in the matter of restriction. The first national immigration law placed a head tax of fifty cents on each new arrival to help meet processing costs and excluded convicts, lunatics, idiots, and those "likely to become a public charge." At the same time, in response to West Coast nativism, Congress passed the Chinese Exclusion Act, but this law stood alone in damming the flood. Three years later, bowing to pressure from labor unions, Congress passed the Foran Act, which prohibited the importation of contract laborers, persons who pledged future wages in return for their passage to the United States. Still, Americans held fast to the ideal that their country's unique mission was to provide a home for the oppressed. It was an article of their faith in democracy and the New World's superiority over Europe. As one advocate of the Foran Act remarked, "This bill in no measure seeks to restrict free immigration; such a proposition would be odious, and justly so, to the American people."

THE GAY NINETIES

Shortly after those brave words were spoken, people began to have second thoughts about the nation's historic immigration policy. This time their doubts were aroused by industrialization. Many Americans were frightened by the economic depressions and social antagonisms accompanying the growth of big business and labor unions. The rise of the city, which they equated with European decadence, also made them uneasy. Unable to cope with these phenomena, many Americans sought a scapegoat on which to vent their frustrations. Immigrants—so closely associated with the problems of modern society that they seemed to cause them—became a prime target.

Nativists singled out the Catholic Church, still synonymous with immigration, as a particular menace. At the end of the nineteenth century Catholic churches were becoming increasingly numerous and their candidates were more successful than ever in local politics, arousing the ire of entrenched Protestant interests. In the late 1880's nativists began to revive the myth that the Pope was trying to take over America. Some foresaw the loss of separation of church and state, while others claimed that the parochial school system was the greatest enemy ever to threaten the American way of life. At this time a number of Americans joined anti-Catholic secret societies, the largest and most powerful of which was the American Protective Association. The A.P.A. was founded in 1887 in the upper Mississippi Valley. It advocated the free public school system as well as a longer naturalization process and drastic immigration restriction. The organization grew slowly until the onset of a serious depression in 1893. Then it quickly gained strength among the unemployed, who were receptive to the A.P.A.'s outlandish claim that the Pope had caused the economic collapse. After a lapse of almost forty years, the same anti-Catholic antagonisms that had swept so many Know-Nothing candidates into office surfaced to give the A.P.A. a membership of well over half a million by 1864. When the economy started to recover, confidence in America returned and the A.P.A. quickly lost support. However, other groups came to look upon immigration restriction as the answer to their own problems.

Organized labor, which had repeatedly complained about the effects of mass immigration on the American workers' standard of living stepped up its protests in the 1890's. Labor unions made much of the fact that immigrants worked for less money than natives and were hard to organize. Actually, as the New York Bureau of Labor noted in 1885, immigrants who were willing to accept very low wages upon arrival quickly became "sufficiently Americanized" to go on strike themselves. And, it might be added, when recruited they became staunch union members. Nevertheless, in 1892 the Knights of Labor called for the exclusion of any immigrant who could not support himself for one year after arrival in America. Five years later the American Federation of Labor came out for restriction of southern and eastern Europeans. Speaking for its members, Samuel Gompers, the A.F. of L.'s president and himself an English Jewish immigrant, wrote, "Cheap labor, ignorant labor, takes our jobs and cuts our wages."

Ironically, while labor criticized immigrants for being docile competitors, businessmen feared them as fomenters of industrial unrest. Taking into account the immigrants' supposed proclivity towards radicalism and lawlessness, management blamed foreign-born unionists for the bitter strikes of the era. Their feelings toward the specifically "new," nonunion immigrants were much more ambivalent. During flush times, employers welcomed the southeastern Europeans for the cheap labor they provided. But during times of depression, when the aliens were a burden to the whole community, businessmen wondered if the money they saved on salaries was worth the high price the country paid in social instability. In arguing for stringent immigration restriction, the general manager of the American Iron and Steel Association claimed that the depression of 1893 was greatly exacerbated by the "presence among us of thousands of idle and vicious foreigners who have not come here to work for a living but to stir up strife and commit crime." When they were not encouraging immigration, the Board of Trade and several other business organizations endorsed these sentiments by officially advocating restriction.

A great variety of fraternal organizations, hereditary patriotic societies and veterans' associations added their voices to the cry for restriction. Many of these groups sprang up in the 1890's to give people the sense of stability they craved. Spouting an exaggerated nationalism, they labelled anything foreign "anti-American." Eventually, their hatred of strangers narrowed down to the newcomers from southeastern Europe, who had the ill-fortune to be entering the country en masse just at that time.

The nativists asserted that the "new" immigrants were mostly male, unskilled "birds of passage" who came to America just to earn money and then returned home when that goal was accomplished. The "old" immigrants, they claimed, had moved to America in families and, looking upon this as their permanent home, quickly spread out over the countryside and mingled with the rest of the population. What the nativists failed to note was that the advance guard of almost every new wave was predominantly male. Moreover, it is almost impossible to make generalizations about the "old" and the "new" immigrants because they were not homogeneous groups. For example, the English and Scandinavians of the "old" tended to return to Europe more frequently than the Armenians and Portuguese of the "new," while the Russian Jews of the "new" group had a higher percentage of skilled laborers than any other nationality except the Scots of the "old" immigration. It was also patently foolish to compare the assimilation of groups who had just arrived with the adjustment of those who had lived in America for decades.

But since the nativists designed their arguments to fulfill emotional needs, they did not probe for errors in their assumptions. After 1910 the theory of the "new" immigrants' inferiority was lent respectability by the 42 volume Dillingham Commission Report. Its "conclusions" were really a compilation of prejudices since they were not borne out by the Commission's own findings.

Of all the organizations which embraced the "inferiority" theory, none was more influential than the Immigration Restriction League. The League was founded in Boston in 1894 by a small group of patricians who resented losing power to the uneducated foreign workers who surrounded and outnumbered them. The League's sole prescription for weeding out the undesirables was a literacy test. Reading a short passage in their own language would not have proved a barrier to northern Europeans, almost all of whom had gone to elementary school. But southern Europeans, who did not yet enjoy the benefits of free education, could be expected to fail. The League's campaign for a literacy test took on the fervor of a crusade to save the "best" people and the "best" things in American life. Over the years its attacks on the "new" immigrants increasingly took on racist overtones. According to Prescott F. Hall, an official of the League, the immigration question came down to whether one wanted America "to be peopled by British, German and Scandinavian stock, historically free, energetic, progressive, or by Slav, Latin and Asiatic races, historically down-trodden, atavistic and stagnant."

In 1895, Henry Cabot Lodge, a League spokesman, introduced a bill to the Senate to exclude any man or woman over the age of fourteen who could not read and write a short passage in any language. The bill passed both houses of Congress, but was vetoed by President Cleveland. The literacy test was reintroduced and passed by Congress on later occasions, only to be similarly killed by Presidents Taft and Wilson. As President Wilson explained his veto in 1915:

In this bill it is proposed to turn away from tests of character and of quality and impose tests which exclude and restrict. . . . Those who come seeking an opportunity are not to be admitted unless they have already had one of the chief opportunities they seek, the opportunity of education. The object of such a provision is restriction, not selection.

But the demand for restriction could not be denied indefinitely. In an atmosphere of high tension brought on by World War I, the nativists mustered enough Congressional votes in 1917 to pass the literacy test over President Wilson's second veto. A corner had been turned in immigration history.

ONE HUNDRED PER CENT AMERICANISM

We are the heirs of all time, and with all nations we divide our inheritance. On this Western Hemisphere all tribes and peoples are forming into one federated whole; and there is a future which shall see the estranged children of Adam restored as to the old hearthstone in [an American] Eden . . . The seed is sown, and the harvest must come.

Thus Herman Melville glorified that mixture of people that was thought to give America its particular genius. Although Melville and his nineteenth-century contemporaries did not use the term "melting pot," they believed implicitly in such a con-

The streets of New York's "Little Italy" comprised
a giant outdoor supermarket. Since they had no
refrigerators, immigrant women went out daily to
buy fresh produce from the pushcart vendors.

cept: that foreigners had only to live in America to become what Crèvecoeur called "the American, this new man." With faith in the automatic nature of assimilation, natives allowed immigrants to adjust to the new environment in their own way. The vigor with which some of the newcomers criticized the nation's materialism and restlessness showed that they did not feel compelled to accept every aspect of the society.

But in the early twentieth century Americans began to lose confidence in the theory that immigrants would automatically become "just like us." After all, the melting pot had been bubbling for a long time and there were still many ethnic enclaves, even among the "old" immigrants. Before, the country was thought to be still developing and diversity was welcomed. Now, afraid of the widening social rifts in their urban-industrial society, Americans wanted unity above all else. Their recipe for turning the newcomer into a "good" American was to have him abandon everything connected with the Old Country, including language, habits and sentimental ties. They expected him to conform completely to a White Anglo-Saxon Protestant way of life that had been defined in advance of his coming. (Reporting on one Italian family's failure to assimilate, a social worker commented, "Not Americanized; still eating spaghetti.")

As World War I loomed in Europe, conformity began to be equated with loyalty. Conversely, diversity began to be considered a threat to the nation. The National Americanization Committee, which started out with the slogan "Many Peoples, But One Nation," symbolically changed its motto to "America First." During the preparedness period, Americanizing the immigrant became a national crusade. Thousands of schools,

churches, civic groups, business organizations, fraternal orders and patriotic societies threw themselves into the task. Often the pressure they exerted on newcomers was of the crudest sort. Anti-Communist business interests gained control of an immigrant press outlet and flooded foreign-language newspapers with patriotic articles and antiradical propaganda. The Daughters of the American Revolution printed a leaflet in fifteen languages admonishing immigrants to respect the Constitution, study American institutions, bank their salaries and desist from dropping trash in the streets. Taking a different tack, liberal Americanizers who supported Wilson's theory of national self-determination asked immigrants to parade in native costume and exhibit their "gifts" to this country while affirming their loyalty.

When Congress declared war the Americanization campaign was stepped up. Suddenly, foreigners and foreign influences became "dangerous"—as they have in every major American conflict starting with the French and Indian Wars. Because Germany was the enemy, Americans singled out German immigrants for especially harsh punishment, although all aliens were suspected of divided loyalties and were treated accordingly. The Cincinnati City Council shut down alien-operated poolrooms on the premise that they kept immigrants from learning the American way of life. The Governor of Iowa went even further and forbade citizens of that state to use any language except English in schools, church services, and even telephone conversations!

Although too short of workers during the war to fire aliens, many manufacturers promoted only citizens or those who had initiated naturalization proceedings. Some employers did their bit for Americanization by enclosing civic lessons in pay envelopes and holding factory classes. Henry Ford, for one, made foreign employees at his automobile plant attend classes before and after work two days a week. Ford's English School was not designed to improve the productivity of workers, but rather to mold them into his idea of the "one hundred per cent American." The first thing that Ford's teachers taught their pupils to say was "I am a good American." Later, the students took part in a performance whose message was so clear no words were needed. In the center of the stage stood a big melting pot, which was so labelled. Into it walked the immigrants, dressed in ridiculous costumes and carrying signs identifying their homelands. At the same time another column of men came out of the melting pot. They were prosperously and identically dressed in standard American business suits and each carried a small American flag.

During the war the immigrants were too overwhelmed by pressure to protest Americanization. They outwardly conformed by going to English classes, marching in parades and showing off their European handicrafts. But once the crisis had subsided they rebelled. The newcomers lashed out at the alternately threatening and patronizing treatment to which they had been subjected, and they hurled invectives at the underlying theme of the campaign: that immigrants were not only different, they were inferior. As an Italian editor succinctly put their reaction, "Americanization is an ugly word."

After the war, some immigrants returned to Europe in a huff, more turned to a compensatory chauvinism such as Zionism. But no matter what their course of action following the Americanization crusade, few could escape a certain amount of self-hatred for being other—and less—than what the majority wanted. Now immigrants were confirmed in their belief that they were not and never could be real Americans. Nor did they think naturalized citizens could accede to that category. Immigrants accepted the larger society's stereotype of the American as someone with English-speaking parents, probably a British-sounding name and a body ideally fitted out with blonde hair, blue eyes and long limbs. They hoped their children would get to mix with real Americans, but they didn't think they themselves could. After World War I, newcomers began to identify themselves as members of minority groups. Although with other "out" people they constituted more than a majority of the population, they used the term "minority" to signify that they had less access to opportunity in the United States than the "in" groups.

THE ROARING TWENTIES

The 1920's are popularly portrayed as a gay era of flappers, dance marathons and bootleg gin, but in reality they were years of fear and disillusionment. The hate-filled spirit of the times was exemplified by the Ku Klux Klan, whose white-robed members rode out at night to frighten and sometimes murder Catholics, Negroes, Jews, or anyone else who didn't conform to their perverted ideas. In all, over three million white Protestant Americans stood before fiery crosses and swore allegiance to the Invisible Empire. During the war Americans had buried their differences in the interests of national unity. But once the conflict was over, opposing interest groups once again clashed violently, threatening the very fabric of American life. The wrangling over the Treaty of Versailles and the League of Nations dissipated America's elation over winning the war. It also led to a revulsion against foreign entanglements abroad and foreign influences at home. Postwar xenophobia struck first at immigrant radicals.

The Communist Revolution in Russia in 1917 and the new activism of radical parties in the United States frightened Americans into thinking that their government, too, might be overthrown. People became further alarmed when violence erupted during the massive textile and steel strikes of 1919. These strikes summoned up the old bogey of the immigrant radical since many of the strikers were foreign-born. Although many natives were involved, too, immigrants were the focus of the "Big Red Scare."

The "Red Scare" was greatly aggravated, if not invented, by Attorney General A. Mitchell Palmer, who told Congress that he knew that the Communists were going "to rise up and destroy the Government at one fell swoop." Backed by public demand for action, Palmer made an initial raid on the radical Union of Russian Workers and had many of the alien members deported. This action proved so popular that he planned another, mightier blow against Communism. On January 2, 1920, the Department of Justice led squads of local police on a mission to ferret out alien members of the Communist Party and the Communist Labor Party. Police officers raided meeting places, pool halls, and private homes in thirty-three cities, taking everyone in sight into custody. The captives were loaded onto trucks or led off handcuffed and chained to one another to be questioned at central meeting points. While many suspected radicals were held for just a few hours, some had to wait several weeks for a hearing. In Detroit eight hundred men were kept penned up in a windowless corridor, surviving solely on the food their families brought in. In all, about three thousand men were tried and hundreds of aliens deported. Yet the Palmer raids were completely illegal. The Secretary of Labor did not declare membership in either Communist party a deportable offense under a 1918 statute until *after* the raids had been completed.

The stereotype of the immigrant criminal was as widely believed as the stereotype of the immigrant radical, and in the early postwar years it was given even more play. Thanks to the lurid imaginations of newspaper editors no group was more closely associated with lawlessness than the Italians. Long before Prohibition, newspapers featured dramatic tales of southern Italian blood feuds and stiletto murders. Indeed, Italian crimes rated so many headlines that Americans began to think of Little Italy as a den of vice. Actually, the first-generation Italians were extremely law-abiding and the second generation committed no more crimes than the average, but, as we have seen before, prejudice maintains a hardy resistance to fact. During the 1920's the movies popularized the stereotype of the Italian mobster that unfortunately remains with us to this day.

Because of their undeserved reputation, Italians suffered beatings, lynchings and, in 1920, this country's worst anti-immigrant riot. This debacle took place in West Frankfort, Illinois, a coal town where workers were temporarily idled by a strike. After a few bank robberies, supposedly engineered by the Italian Mafia, two boys were kidnapped and found dead. Jumping to the "logical" conclusion that Italians were behind the murders, mobs stormed the town's Italian section, brutally clubbing its inhabitants and setting fire to their homes. Despite the presence of five hundred state troopers, West Frankfort was in an uproar for three days.

While Jews were never subjected to the kind of violence Italians faced at West Frankfort, they were the victims of a more thoroughgoing discrimination. From colonial times until the end of the nineteenth century, the Jewish population of the United States remained small and practically indistinguishable from the rest of the American people. Then, between 1880 and 1914, when the influx from eastern Europe was at its height, the number of Jews in America leaped from about three hundred thousand to over four million. Suddenly Jews became very conspicuous and their exceptionally swift upward mobility quickly brought them into contact with American society. Starting in the 1890's the designation "Jew" began to carry with it a social stigma. Those professing the religion were increasingly barred from summer resorts, social clubs, and better residential neighborhoods. Then, in the 1920's, private schools and universities instituted strict quotas to keep out Jewish newcomers lest the places of learning become, as some Harvard students feared, a "new Jerusalem." Discrimination proceeded apace in the business world and by the end of the decade an estimated 90 per cent of New York's white collar jobs were closed to Jews.

Criticism of Jews centered around two stereotypes: the Jewish radical who imported the ideas of the Russian Revolution and the Jewish banker who controlled the American economy. Intellectually these two images conflicted, but emotionally they resolved themselves in the over-all menace of the international

Jew. The tens of thousands of Jewish refugees pouring through Ellis Island, just when the country was undergoing a severe depression, made the Jewish "threat" seem very real. Leading the smear campaign against the Jews was Henry Ford, an American hero. Americans looked up to the "Flivver King" as the symbol of a simpler, happier time. To them he combined the settler's rugged individualism, the country boy's distrust of the big city, and the tinkerer's knack for practical solutions. Ford was also a rabid anti-Semite. In 1920 his newspaper, *The Dearborn Independent,* began a series of violent attacks on Jews, which was closely followed around the country and which met with much whispered approval.

Those people who were receptive to outrageous lies about "new" immigrants usually believed in superior and inferior races of men. White America had long been accustomed to ascribing certain unfavorable characteristics to black and yellow men on the basis of skin color; now it simply extended those prejudices to include certain white people, too. Indeed, in the 1920's before Hitler raised the banner of a superior Aryan race in Germany, the self-serving notion of superior and inferior races of white men enjoyed a great vogue in the United States.

The most famous spokesman for the racist school of thought was Madison Grant, the patrician trustee of the American Museum of Natural History and chairman of the New York Zoological Society. In his book, *The Passing of the Great Race,* Grant glorified the earlier Anglo-Saxon or Nordic settler with "his stature, his light colored eyes, his fair skin and light colored hair, his straight nose and his splendid fighting and moral qualities." Correspondingly, he deplored the influx of the new immigrants,

[*177*]

"the lowest and most primitive elements." Many respectable publications including the most widely read magazine of its day, *The Saturday Evening Post,* quoted and commended Grant. The *Post* also published a series of articles by Kenneth L. Roberts which was later published as a book, *Why Europe Leaves Home*. Roberts asserted:

The American nation was founded and developed by the Nordic race, but if a few more million members of the Alpine, Mediterranean, and Semitic races are poured among us, the result must inevitably be a hybrid race of people as worthless and futile as the good-for-nothing mongrels of Central America and Southwestern Europe.

"Proof" of the inferiority of the "new" immigrants was provided by the intelligence tests used by the Army for the first time during World War I. Soldiers from southern and eastern Europe scored markedly lower than those from northern and western Europe. It later became clear that the I.Q. scores reflected cultural and educational backgrounds, not intelligence, but by then the damage had been done. During the twenties, the pseudo-scientific eugenics movement, which was concerned with proper breeding among human beings, also lent racism intellectual respectability.

Ultimately, racist thinking turned out to be the single most important factor in restricting immigration. If, as nativists argued, the "new" immigrants were too biologically inferior to understand American institutions, then no amount of "Americanizing" would do any good. With rehabilitation thus discredited the only alternative was rejection.

✒ END OF AN ERA

As a pilgrim father that missed th' first boat, I must raise me claryon voice again' th' invasion iv this fair land be th' paupers an' arnychists in Europe. Ye bet I must—because I'm here first. . . . In thim days America was th' refuge iv th' oppressed in all th' wurruld. . . . But as I tell ye, 'tis diff'rent now. 'Tis time we put our back again' th' open dure an' keep out th' savage horde.

—Mr. Dooley

At the turn of the century, Mr. Dooley, the Irish bartender created for the newspapers by Finley Peter Dunne commented ironically on the idea of restriction, and many Americans chuckled along with him. But in 1920 restriction was no longer a laughing matter. The literacy test was proving a great disappointment to its promoters because southern and eastern Europeans had heard all about the test and came thoroughly prepared for it. When commercial shipping resumed after the war, the number of immigrants passing through Ellis Island approached prewar proportions—and the overwhelming majority was still from southern and eastern Europe. Fearing that the United States would be deluged by starving Europeans at a time when so many natives were out of work, Americans set up a clamor for immigration restriction.

In 1921 Congress acceded to the public demand by passing a temporary restriction law. Although designed only as a stopgap measure, this statute actually set the pattern for the next forty-four years of immigration legislation. It inaugurated the "national origins" concept that a man's place of birth is the most important factor in determining the kind of citizen he will make. Under the law a quota was assigned to each European country in proportion to the number of immigrants from that country already living in the United States in 1910. Since most of the foreign-born in 1910 were "old" immigrants, this formula clearly discriminated in favor of northern and western Europeans. In all, about three hundred and fifty thousand newcomers were to be permitted entry each year, far less than the annual number of arrivals before World War I. The 1921 statute also marked the first time a numerical limit was set on immigration.

Three years later Congress passed the Johnson-Reed Act, which went into effect fully in 1929. The Act set no limit on immigration from our "Good Neighbors" in the Western Hemisphere, but it reduced the total quota for Europe to one hundred and fifty thousand a year. It also changed the basis of quota assignment from the national origins of the foreign-born in 1910 to the national origins of the entire white population, foreign- and native-born, in 1920. According to the new formula, over 80 per cent of the quota places were allocated to the countries of northwestern Europe, with Great Britain still claiming the lion's share. As if the racist intent of the Johnson-Reed Act were not blatant enough, the law went on to bar any but white immigrants from Asia and Africa.

This time Congress did its work well, for the Act effectively damned the flood from southern and eastern Europe and reduced immigration to a trickle. With the law's passage an era came to an end. Three hundred years of free immigration were over.

* * *

At no time did immigrants let the crusade for restriction go unopposed. From the first, the entire foreign-language press had bitterly denounced the literacy test proposal and in 1898 several ethnic groups joined forces in the Immigration Protective League. After the turn of the century every national society from the great German-American Alliance to tiny Finnish social clubs sent around petitions, held meetings, and testified before Congressional committees in an effort to keep the gates open. The ardor of northwestern Europeans dampened after World War I, when they saw that new legislation would not be aimed at them. Most "old" groups simply dropped out of the fight, but some Scandinavians went so far as to enthusiastically endorse greater restriction of the southern and eastern Europeans.

The "new" immigrants tried to rouse public sympathy for their cause by reminding Americans of the nation's cosmopolitan past and its historic mission of asylum. Horace Kallen, a Jewish writer, postulated the then startling concept of "cultural pluralism"—that the true idea of America lies in fostering ethnic differences, not in blending them in the melting pot. But spokesmen for the "new" immigrants had little impact on public opinion. Nor did their lobbyists make any headway with members of Congress. Although the immigrant vote was significant, it didn't compare to the combined power of all the groups promoting restriction. At the last minute immigrant leaders begged for an audience with President Calvin Coolidge to persuade him to veto the Johnson-Reed Act. He refused to see them.

Until World War I, immigrants could still cling to the illusion that a policeman's slight, a social worker's patronizing tone, or even a mob's violence was nothing more than an isolated unpleasantry. But when discriminatory restriction became the law of the land, immigrants could no longer fool themselves about

America's real opinion of them. It was obvious that most natives didn't want any more "new" immigrants because they didn't like the ones they already had. Deeply stung, some immigrants reacted by seeking a colonial past for their group or by turning against a minority with even lower status than their own. A great number clung more tightly than ever to their ghettos, where people spoke their language and nobody made fun of them.

But the ghetto was doomed. Without reinforcements from Europe, Americanization among the various groups accelerated and many ethnic institutions lost their original purpose. In the 1920's movies and radio drew audiences away from the immigrant theater just as picture newspapers drew readers away from the immigrant press. In the 1930's the Depression caused many immigrant organizations to declare bankruptcy and close their doors. At the same time immigrants were deserting the ghetto in droves. By 1926 some two hundred thousand Jews had moved out of the Lower East Side to less crowded city neighborhoods or to the suburbs. The Italians followed suit and by 1940 more than half of New York's Italian-born population lived outside so-called Italian neighborhoods. Poles, Czechs, Greeks and other groups in other cities showed the same tendency to disperse.

In any case, the ghetto was destined to be essentially a one-generation phenomenon. Public schools began turning the children of immigrants into "Americans" when they were only five or six years old. Soon the youngsters were more interested in dressing and acting like their contemporaries than in emulating their "old-fashioned" parents. As the second generation grew up and entered American life, the generation gap widened still fur-

Under the influence of a public school education,
immigrant children quickly became Americanized.
But their new standards of behavior often
brought them into conflict with their parents.

ther. Finally, the immigrants' attachment to the Old Country and its ways became boring, if not embarrassing, to their offspring.

One can still discern ethnic groups within the American population, but each year they diminish in size and vigor. Affiliation with an organized religious group has taken the place of ethnic identification, and churches and temples have become the focus of group activity rather than the immigrant lodge. Moreover, a common religion, rather than a common European background, is now the general framework within which people tend to marry. Today, except for the larger division of black and white, the designations Protestant, Catholic and Jew are the most meaningful distinctions within our society.

❧ POSTSCRIPT

During the Depression the lack of available jobs combined with a strict interpretation of the Johnson-Reed Act resulted in a drastic curtailment of immigration. In fact, there were some years when more people left the country than entered it. In the twenty-five years after "national origins" went into effect, the net gain from immigration was less than that of the single year, 1907. The greatest losers from the Government's strict interpretation of the Johnson-Reed Act were those Germans who wanted to flee the Nazi regime. Only two hundred and fifty thousand were able to reach the safety of the United States—and these were admitted under the German quota. Interestingly, the Government showed more compassion at the height of nativism in 1917 when, in the interest of Russian Jews, Congress exempted those fleeing religious persecution from taking the literacy test. In 1948 Congress passed the Displaced Persons Act, authorizing some four hundred thousand homeless people to settle in the United States. However, the D.P.'s too were charged to the quotas of their country of origin.

During the Administration of Harry S. Truman, Congress thoroughly reviewed the nation's immigration policy and in 1952 it passed the Immigration and Nationality Act over the President's veto. This law, better known as the McCarran-Walter Act, removed the ban on Asian and African immigrants and permitted spouses and minor children of citizens to enter as nonquota immigrants. But it extended practically intact the national origins quota system. Immediately after the McCarran-Walter Act was passed a barrage of criticism was leveled against its racist and inequitable provisions. Immigrant leaders pointed out that because quotas were not transferable, Great Britain was using only half her allotment of sixty-five thousand slots while Italy had a twenty-year waiting list for its five and a half thousand places. Critics also charged that the quota system was an insult to the emerging nations of Africa and Asia, which received only token quotas of one hundred each.

Upon taking office, President Kennedy initiated legislation to substitute general priorities for the national origins quota system. He was motivated not only by the desire to remove the racial stain from our laws but also by the wish to make immigration policy more responsive to the country's manpower needs. The President's plan was set forth in the popular little book, *A Nation of Immigrants,* which was published after his death. Although President Kennedy was unable to get his reform bill through

Congress, President Johnson gave the measure top priority and met with success. After Congress passed the immigration bill in 1965, the President flew to New York to sign it into law at the Statue of Liberty. He hailed the demise of the national origins quota system, which he termed "incompatible with our basic American traditions."

Under the new immigration and nationality act, one hundred and seventy thousand immigrants a year may enter from the Eastern Hemisphere, with no one country to exceed twenty thousand. Seventy-four per cent of the quota places are set aside for family relationships, 20 per cent for professionals, skilled and unskilled persons who fill a specified need in the economy, and 6 per cent for refugees and others who don't fit into one of the major categories. Husbands, wives, children and parents of citizens come in as nonquota immigrants, while Cuban refugees are admitted under a separate law. The 1965 statute also imposes the first limit on arrivals from the Western Hemisphere. One hundred and twenty thousand of our neighbors may enter on a first-come, first-served basis.

Although the effects of the new law are just beginning to be felt, it is already apparent that a dramatic shift is taking place in the source of immigration. In the same period British immigration dropped from twenty-seven to seven thousand, while Italian immigration shot up from ten to twenty-six thousand. And, whereas the typical newcomer of the past was a peasant with few occupational or educational skills, the newest additions to our population may well be the cream of their country's educated class. In fact, some nations are already complaining about an acceleration of the "brain drain" in which their most valuable personnel leave for the

The Johnson-Reed Act of 1924 rang down the curtain on 300 years of unrestricted immigration. Although modifications have been made in the law, it is still true that only a certain number of newcomers may enter the country each year.
GEORGE EASTMAN HOUSE COLLECTION

United States, where they can earn higher salaries. Although a backlog from the old quota system has temporarily raised immigration figures, some observers fear that the ultimate result of the new law will be to stifle, rather than encourage, immigration. They see potential obstacles in the new quotas for the Western Hemisphere and the stiff requirements and red tape involved in importing labor. One immigration lawyer interviewed by the *Christian Science Monitor* recently said she was not certain just how the new regulations would work out. "But," she affirmed, "it will be a different crowd coming now."

The text visible within the cartoon:

"COOLIE, SLAVE, PAUPER AND RAT-EATER."

THE CHINESE QUESTION.

"THE CHINAMAN WORKS CHEAP BECAUSE HE IS A BARBARIAN AND SEEKS GRATIFICATION OF ONLY THE LOWEST, THE MOST INEVITABLE WANTS." —WENDELL PHILLIPS.

"THE LOWEST AND VILEST OF THE HUMAN RACE.

I (A WHITE MAN) AM OPPOSED TO HIM ON GROUNDS OF —
1, RACE; 2, INDUSTRY; 3, POLITICS; 4, MORALITY.

TRADES — UNIONS. MEETING

"RESOLVED,

IMPORTATION OF CHINESE BARBARIANS IN TO THE COUNTRY MUST BE STOPPED BY THE BALLOT OR BULLET." —WORKINGMEN.(?)

"THEY ARE DISHONEST AND FALSE, VICIOUS, IMMORAL AND HEATHENISH."
"HEATHEN IMMORALITY OF THE CHINESE RACE IS BEYOND DESCRIPTION

"DEGRADED LABOR OF ASIA"
"EUROPEAN IMMORALITY IS VIRTUE ITSELF WHEN COMPARED WITH CHINESE IMMORALITY"

JOHN CHINAMAN IS AN IDOLATER AND HEATHEN"

"SERVILE LABORERS FROM ASIA" JOSS HOUSES IN OUR MIDST

CHINESE PAGANISM HAS, BY ITS FRUITS A PRACTICAL IMMORALITY FOULER FAR THAN THAT KNOWN AMONG ANY EUROPEAN OR CHRISTIAN PEOPLE."

NO FAMILY! VIRTUES SUCH AS WE HAVE" (WHITE PURITY)

COLORED ORPHAN ASYLUM

IF OUR BALLOT WILL NOT STOP THEM COMING WE RULE IT BY OUR COUNTRY THE BULLET MUST

Th. Nast.

In this cartoon the figure representing the spirit of America declares, "America Means Fair Play For All Men." But the vicious mobs who repeatedly attacked Chinese immigrants went unpunished. CHICAGO HISTORICAL SOCIETY

The Pacific Migration

I~N 1782 HECTOR ST. JOHN CRÈVECOEUR~ defined an American as "either an European, or the descendant of an European," and the definition stuck. Of course, no one can dispute the Europeans' contribution to populating the country, transforming the wilderness, and founding the new country. But from the beginning there were others who made contributions and also deserved to be called "Americans." Crèvecoeur simply left out Africans, thereby denying the existence of 20 per cent of the population at that time. Over the years, the Frenchman's European-American prototype continued to be widely accepted, but it became even more inaccurate as men journeyed eastward from Asia and northward from Latin America.

Of the three non-Continental immigrant groups, the Orientals were most like their European counterparts. They performed the same economic functions and adjusted to American life through the same type of organizations. They even moved for the same reason: economic improvement. The desire among certain Chinese to literally "strike it rich" set in motion a Pacific migration which has brought over four hundred thousand Chinese and three hundred and fifty thousand Japanese to the United States.

✌ GOLD!

Gold! Free gold for anyone who would mine it! Gold nuggets as big as a man's fist lying in shallow rivers! All along China's coasts foreign sailors carried news of the gold strike at Sutter's Mill, California, in January 1848, and with each retelling the size of the nuggets and the gold fields got bigger and bigger. Throughout China people were excited by the idea of free gold, but, although the country was poor and overpopulated, the peasants did not consider pulling up stakes to go prospecting. For one thing, the Chinese family was one of the most tightly knit in the world and men did not leave home easily. For another, the average peasant had so little knowledge of the outside world that he could not imagine another life for himself beside his present one of unending work. Only in southeastern China, particularly in the province of Kwantung, did men act upon the news of Sutter's Mill. Historically the people of this area had had the most exposure to Westerners through the nearby ports of Hong Kong and Canton, and they were the least afraid of leaving the Middle Kingdom. Indeed, they already formed the majority of China's expatriates, called Overseas Chinese, in Southeast Asia.

News of the gold discovery at Sutter's mill drew
flocks of natives and foreigners to California,
where they hoped to "strike it rich." In fact, very
few became wealthy panning for gold.

Before a man could strike out for California, he had to scrape together the passage money, but few peasants could finance the three-month crossing themselves. Very often relatives contributed to the sailing fund, pawning jewelry and selling farm animals in hopes that the Argonaut, or gold-seeker, would make their fortunes. In China emigration was a crime punishable by death, but through delicate negotiation port officials could always be bribed. After the requisite sum of money changed hands, the Argonaut was smuggled onto the hold of a foreign ship, where, tightly packed together with other men on a straw mat, he crossed the seven thousand miles of Pacific Ocean separating Kwantung from California.

Upon landing in San Francisco, the first Chinese Argonauts followed more experienced natives and Europeans into the surrounding hills to pan for gold. As more Chinese began to arrive, the firstcomers formed an immigration agency to protect their interests. The Chinese Six Companies, as they called their group after the six districts from which most came, performed many of the services of the Italian padrone. It advanced newcomers the money to pay for picks, shovels and other mining supplies and it directed the men to fields where assistants were needed. The apprenticeship system was mutually beneficial to Chinese and Caucasians. Under it, Chinese greenhorns learned the techniques of mining, while keeping half the gold they found. The white men for whom they worked profited in higher yields, because the Orientals patiently sifted out small particles of gold dust that other forty-niners overlooked.

The packets of gold dust and nuggets that Argonauts sent home to their families created a sensation in China, and the

The first Chinese Argonauts assisted more
experienced men in their mining operations. Since
the Orientals patiently sifted out the smallest
particles of gold, they were highly valued as
apprentices. CALIFORNIA STATE LIBRARY

Chinese began to call America *Gum Shan,* "Mountain of Gold."
So dazzling were the prospects of more riches to follow that girls
considered themselves lucky to marry into a family with one
member in California. As "America fever" swept Kwantung, immigration snowballed. Remittances in "America letters" financed
the journey for some, and family contributions made up the passage for the rest. Within four years of Sutter's Mill there were
twenty-five thousand Chinese in California and by 1880 that
figure had quadrupled. In the beginning the Orientals looked
upon the United States only as a place to make quick money;
China was still "home." American economic opportunities, however, caused a great many newcomers to prolong their temporary
visits into life-long stays. From the gold fields the Chinese first
branched out into personal services.

LAUNDRIES, RAILROADS AND RECLAMATION

Since few women of any nationality, American included, accompanied men to the mineral fields, family life was almost non-existent in the early days of the far West. In 1850, women accounted for only 8 per cent of the population of California and only 2 per cent in the mining counties. Without their wives or mothers, the men were much more dependent on laundries, tailor shops and restaurants. But few Argonauts wanted to take time out from their prospecting to staff these establishments, and, in any case, they looked down upon personal services, considering them "women's work." As a result miners had to send their dirty shirts to Hawaii or Canton and wait months for their return or pay up to eight dollars a dozen to have their shirts laundered locally. The Chinese had as little experience with, or affinity for, "women's work" as the other miners, but they quickly recognized its economic potential.

The Chinese saw the same advantages in the laundry business, for example, that eastern European Jews saw in the garment trades: little capital was needed to set up shop and one prospered in direct proportion to how hard he worked. With soap, a scrub board, an iron, and ironing board the Chinese immigrant became an entrepreneur. Moreover, since he picked up and delivered the garments himself, he did not have to pay high rentals for an attractive shop in a good neighborhood. The Chinese looked upon laundering as menial work to be endured for the sake of the rice bowl, but, in fact, it served them well. Later on, when widespread discrimination barred them from almost every other field, laundries provided them with a secure niche in the economy.

[*194*]

Although greater capital was required to start restaurants than laundries, the number of Chinese employed in both fields was about equal. Some Chinese who started out as company cooks and domestic servants went on to open their own restaurants. These establishments were quite popular along the mining frontier, where they specialized in hearty dinners and lunch pail fillers. Chop suey and chow mein, two of the most well-known "Chinese" dishes in America were probably developed in this era to satisfy the miners' desire for a lot of food at a low price. In any case, these specialties were definitely "made in America" because they were completely unknown in China.

During the Civil War the Central Pacific Railroad approached the Chinese Six Companies for workers. This was a last resort for the Railroad, which had found few white men interested in hard, manual labor. Indeed, the few white men who did report for work on the line quit as soon as they earned the stage fare to Virginia City, the site of new mineral discoveries. But the Chinese felt very differently about the chance to earn $35 a month. The Six Companies had no trouble recruiting them in either the United States or southern China, where rebellion was paralyzing the economy. Of the ten thousand men who built the Union Pacific, nine thousand were Chinese. Their contribution to the transcontinental railroad was rivaled only by that of the Irish, who worked westward on the Union Pacific. At first the Central Pacific's officers were skeptical about the Chinese's ability to handle the job, but they soon praised the immigrants' bravery and competence. During the winter of 1865–1866 three thousand workmen lived and carried out their jobs in tunnels dug beneath forty-foot snow drifts. The following summer six thousand Chinese threaded their way along precarious ledges pushing heavy wheel-barrow loads of debris or balancing seventy-pound powder kegs on the ends of bamboo poles. Nothing seemed to faze these men, not even working from small baskets suspended one thousand feet above the ground.

When the Central Pacific met the Union Pacific at Ogden, Utah, in 1869, thousands of Chinese were thrown out of work. Unemployment was temporary, however, for the Chinese were soon recruited to fill in other gaps in the labor force. Some went to work in mines, and cigar and woolen factories, jobs scorned by white men looking for fast, easy money. Others went into California's burgeoning agricultural industry. Farmers in California simply could not find enough white field hands, even when they offered to pay them the then exorbitant wages of $2.50 a day. Moreover, the farmers complained that the men who would work spoiled a great deal of produce by rough han-dling. In desperation, some owners hired a few Chinese to pick fruits and vegetables. The Orientals proved to be such diligent and careful workers that growers were soon seeking them out in great numbers. In 1870 the Chinese constituted about one-tenth of California's farm workers, while fourteen years later they ac-counted for fully half the state's agricultural force—a percentage out of all proportion to their numbers.

In addition to cultivating existing farm lands, the Chinese created whole new agricultural areas. Standing in water up to their waists, they dug ditches and raised dikes at the mouths of the San Joaquin and Sacramento Rivers. Eventually they re-claimed five million acres of the richest farm land in the state, a truly remarkable accomplishment considering that they used no machinery. The Orientals were also prominent on road gangs and other public work projects. Historians agree that the Chinese, more than any other single group, laid the basis for California's growth from a rag-tag collection of mining camps to a varied and thriving economic community.

"THE CHINESE MUST GO!"

In the beginning the Chinese were accepted as just a slightly more exotic addition to the mixture of adventurers, farm boys, and gunslingers who flocked into western mining camps. Local accounts of the celebrations marking California's admittance to the Union in 1850 mention that the Chinese figured prominently in the festivities. The San Francisco newspaper, *Alta California,* declared, "The China Boys will yet vote at the same polls, study at the same schools, and bow at the same altar as our countrymen." In 1852 the state's governor called for land grants to encourage the continued immigration and settlement of the Chinese, whom he termed, "one of the most worthy of our newly adopted citizens." Yet when the economy collapsed twenty years later, this early reservoir of good will toward the Chinese vanished.

Until the panic of 1873, California enjoyed a booming, if unstable, prosperity. Mining, the Civil War, and construction of the Central Pacific inflated prices completely out of proportion to real worth. Californians gambled recklessly in mining stocks and, when the stock market failed, almost everyone was hit hard. The savage depression which ensued aggravated an already volatile social situation, because California was then home to thousands of unemployed railroad workers and drifters who had been attracted to the West by its get-rich-quick reputation. Unwilling to accept the fact that the boom days were over, these rootless people, instead, sought a scapegoat on which to vent their frustrations.

The Chinese, with their queues, pajamas, and distinctive facial features, made easy targets for the bullyboys. Moreover, they were numerous enough to seem like a threat. Typically, the Orientals were blamed for accepting low wages and taking jobs away from white workers. In reality, of course, they presented little competition because they did work no white man would do. Caucasians ridiculed their eating habits, their social customs, and their "heathen idols." But most pernicious of all, nativists insisted that the Chinese inherited along with their yellow skin a "backwardness" that would forever prevent them from assimilating. This line of reasoning, which was used so effectively against "new" immigrants in later years, was employed by many southerners who had moved westward with all their prejudices intact. They made sure that the Chinese were considered a "colored" and, therefore, inferior, race in the West.

Lurid newspaper tales and sensational cheap novels laid the basis for America's wholly inaccurate concept of the Chinese. Starting with some vague notions of the "mysterious" Orient, natives began to imagine that every meek laundryman was really a white slaver, a murdering thief or an opium addict. No matter that the Chinese were generally a hard-working, scrupulously law-abiding people and that Chinatown was really a tame, rather ordinary neighborhood. The aura of "evil" simply could not be shaken. One of the most popular poems of its day was Bret

Harte's tale of Ah Sin, the Chinese who turns the tables on a white man who has been trying to cheat him at cards. Harte's "Plain Language from Truthful James," popularly known as "The Heathen Chinee," was copied by every newspaper from San Francisco to New York shortly after its publication in 1871. People carried the poem around with them and the most significant lines were read and applauded in the House of Representatives. Harte wrote, in part:

> Then I looked up at Nye,
>   And he gazed upon me;
> And he rose with a sigh,
>   And said, "Can this be?
> We are ruined by Chinese cheap labor,"
>   And he went for that heathen Chinee.
>
> Which is why I remark,
>   And my language is plain,
> That for ways that are dark
>   And for tricks that are vain,
> The heathen Chinee is peculiar,
>   Which the same I am free to maintain.

At this time "anti-coolie" clubs, such as "The Order of Caucasians," began to agitate against the Chinese. Then trade union leaders, recognizing a sure way to gain popularity, took up the cause. One of the worst demagogues was Dennis Kearney, who wielded considerable power through the Workingmen's Party. Kearney, a recently naturalized citizen from Ireland, advocated a daily wage of four dollars and a roast beef dinner for every laborer. San Francisco newspapers vied with one another in giving Kearney publicity and soon politicians of every party were taking up his inflammatory cry, "The Chinese must go!" Some of the most vicious attacks were mounted by Irish unionists. It is ironic, but not without parallel in American history, that a group still suffering from discrimination in the East was rallying to save the Union from "foreigners" in the West.

Through a great deal of high-pressure lobbying, the trade unionists convinced the California state legislature to bar "Mongolians" from jobs in private corporations and public projects. Soon many other western states were passing equally discriminatory laws including a ban on intermarriage between Orientals and members of other races. Unionists organized boycotts against shopkeepers, growers, and manufacturers who employed Orientals. To protect themselves, businessmen began to display signs reading, "We employ no Chinese labor here." Finally, discrimination became so widespread that the Orientals found they could neither eat in a white restaurant nor rent a place to live outside of Chinatown.

It was almost inevitable that antipathy as strong as that toward the Chinese would go beyond legal channels and erupt into violence—a violence far more extreme than any previous anti-European outbursts. In the 1850's and 1860's there had been a few isolated anti-Chinese incidents, but brutal attacks now became widespread. When the inhabitants of San Francisco's Chinatown strayed beyond its confines they were subject to stoning, assault, robbery, and even murder. In July 1877 mobs burned down twenty-five wash houses in the city and for months afterwards there was sporadic rioting. In 1885 in Rock Springs, Wyoming, twenty-eight Chinese were massacred and hundreds more wounded and driven from their homes. The following year in Log Cabin, Oregon, a similar purge took place. Throughout these years of humiliation and terror the Chinese were never given police protection nor was their testimony accorded any validity in court. Significantly the phrase "not a Chinaman's chance" came into our language at this time.

The Chinese could find no politician to champion their cause because they had no votes to offer in exchange for his favors. They were aliens and seemed destined to remain so. Under the original naturalization law of 1790 only "free white persons" were entitled to citizenship. Although the law's framers intended that phrase to exclude only slaves and Indians living in tribes, later generations gave it a racial interpretation. After the Civil War persons of African descent were allowed to become citizens, but West Coast forces saw to it that the original restriction was continued for Orientals. The Chinese and later the Japanese bitterly resented their ineligible-for-citizenship status, especially when it was used to discriminate against and exclude them.

The ultimate goal of the anti-Chinese factions was complete exclusion and they worked tirelessly to attain it. For years the Chinese had freely entered the United States under the Reed Treaty of 1858 and the Burlingame Treaty of 1868. Then in 1882 a coalition of southern and western racists pushed through the Chinese Exclusion Act barring Chinese laborers for a period of ten years. This law was followed by even more restrictive legislation. Still the nativists did not stop until they had passed the Johnson-Reed Act of 1924, which totally prohibited the immigration of any persons "ineligible to citizenship." Because of this insensitive ruling many wives were stranded in China and the "fractured family" became commonplace in the Chinese community. Moreover, since there were very few single Chinese women in the United States, the law condemned male immigrants to bachelorhood or to intermarriage which entailed a great deal of social ostracism. As applied to the Chinese then, the Johnson-Reed Act was not merely exclusionary, it was punitive.

Through an accident of history a certain number of Chinese managed to immigrate to the United States in spite of exclusion. The San Francisco earthquake of 1906 destroyed all city records, thereby making birthplaces impossible to validate. Suddenly many Chinese decided that they had been born in America. As citizens they were free to bring in their children and many did import their real offspring, but others took advantage of the situation to bring in "paper sons" for a fee. However, "paper sons" were never very numerous and after the Exclusion Act of 1882 more Chinese left the country than entered it. In typical immigrant fashion, the Chinese who remained in the United States began to demand higher wages. Faced with a shortage of cheap labor and a rapidly expanding agriculture, California growers began to cast around for another group to replace the Chinese. Their search took them to Japan.

~€ JAPANESE ENTERPRISE

Beginning in the 1850's American sugar and pineapple planters in Hawaii petitioned the Emperor of Japan for the right to hire

his subjects as contract laborers, but they were consistently refused. Then, in 1885, the Mikado took notice of the extreme
overcrowding on Japan's rocky islands and reversed his position.
He decided to encourage those from the most densely populated
areas to leave. The first contract laborers departed from the cities
of Tokyo and Yokohama, while later emigrants left from the
southern end of Honshu and the northern region of Kyushu. So
delighted were the Hawaiians to receive these new workers that
King Kalahaua himself went down to the dock to welcome the
first boatload with a speech in carefully memorized Japanese.

For many workers Hawaii proved to be just a stepping stone
to the American mainland and by 1910 over seventy thousand
Japanese had reached our Pacific Coast. They congregated mainly
in California, where they took jobs in canneries, lumber camps,
private households, and on railroads and farms. In agriculture
the Japanese picked up where the Chinese had left off—as
mobile, seasonal field hands. But, unlike the Chinese, who
showed no interest in becoming landowners, most Japanese were
not content to remain migratory workers for long. After a few
years in the United States they bought or leased marginal lands
no one else wanted and built them into prosperous farms. As
early as 1920 the Japanese owned nearly seventy-five thousand
acres of farmland and leased almost four hundred thousand
more. Only 2 per cent of California's population, they produced
13 per cent of its agricultural goods. The Japanese reaped more
from poor lands than Caucasians did from far richer soil because they brought over intensive farming techniques and experimented with new scientific methods. Moreover, they worked
much harder than their American counterparts. Like eastern

European immigrants in the garment trades, the Japanese got ahead, in part, by exploiting their families, their low-paid assistants and, above all, themselves.

The Japanese carved out a special niche for themselves by cultivating strawberries, lettuce, and other low-growing crops that required stoop labor, backbreaking work no Caucasian would do. They were also the first to plant rice on the West Coast. When white men refused to sell their produce, some of the Orientals became wholesalers and retailers in order to furnish outlets for their countrymen's products. This network operated so efficiently that the Japanese became the sole handlers of certain fruits, flowers, and vegetables from "sowing to sale." In all its various phases, then, agriculture made the Japanese as economically independent as the laundry business made the Chinese.

In Hawaii, California, Oregon, and Washington many Japanese also earned their livelihood in the fishing and canning industries. One of their most outstanding successes was Terminal Island in Los Angeles harbor. Japanese fishermen established a thriving business in tuna and sardines here in 1901. Not content with merely catching the fish, they soon built canneries to process it, thereby creating employment opportunities for others—Japanese and Caucasian. By 1942 Terminal Island, 60 per cent of its population of Japanese origin, was furnishing most of the seafood for the city of Los Angeles.

Instead of applauding the Japanese for their enterprise, Californians attacked them. Large growers did not like to see their main source of cheap labor disappear and small growers were afraid of the formidable competition the Orientals presented. "What can we do to protect ourselves when thrift, good farming and foresightedness turn out that way?" complained the *Pacific Rural Press* in 1906. It did not take long for Californians to think up an answer. In 1913 growers convinced the state legislature to pass the Alien Land Act forbidding "aliens ineligible for citizenship" to own agricultural land or to lease it for more than three years at a time. The state also passed a law preventing the Japanese immigrants from obtaining commercial fishing licenses. Rather than give up everything they had worked so hard for, the Japanese circumvented these laws. In some instances they took out deeds in the name of their American-born children, the Nisei, who were citizens; in other cases they formed partnerships with natives and used their names on official papers. Through these methods, the Japanese successfully blunted the economic impact of the alien land and fishing laws, but they were still vulnerable to the psychological impact. Along with discrimination by labor unions, employers, landlords, and operators of public facilities, these statutes were a constant reminder to the Japanese of their second-class status in America.

A GENTLEMEN'S AGREEMENT

Already conditioned to hate Orientals, many Californians easily transferred their prejudices from the Chinese to the Japanese. Actually, most people simply confused the two. Ironically, when Caucasians did sort them out, they complimented the recently despised Chinese as "faithful laborers [who] do not buy land." Agitation against the Japanese was led by organized labor, nativist groups, and circulation-seeking newspapers who dusted off all their old arguments against the Chinese and reused them practically verbatim.

In February 1905, the *San Francisco Chronicle* kicked off the hate campaign with a series of sensational articles including: "JAPANESE A MENACE TO AMERICAN WOMEN," "CRIME AND POVERTY GO HAND IN HAND WITH ASIATIC LABOR" and "BROWN ASIATICS STEAL BRAINS OF WHITES." These articles were quickly followed by the formation of the Japanese and Korean Exclusion League, which attracted almost eighty thousand members within a year. The stories also prompted the California state legislature to unanimously approve a resolution asking Congress to exclude Japanese immigrants.

Anti-Japanese hostility continued to mount and occasionally manifested itself in personal assaults on the Orientals. Then in the fall of 1906 the San Francisco Board of Education ordered all Japanese students to attend a segregated school. The board claimed that the move was necessary to ease overcrowding. Since only ninety-three pupils—twenty-five of them American-born—were Japanese out of the city's student body of twenty-five thousand, this explanation was patently ridiculous. The board also charged that Japanese students were "corrupting" white pupils, although not one white parent had lodged a complaint to this effect. The school board's action was engineered by Mayor Schmitz, who needed an issue to take the spotlight off his imminent indictment for corruption. The school ploy worked perfectly. After the Japanese government lodged a strong protest and crowds in Japan demonstrated against the board's action, California politicians began to rally the people for war. At one mass meeting Mayor Schmitz volunteered to lay down his life in battle against the Japanese, a statement which prompted the *Los Angeles Times* to remark: "It is a notable fact that his Honor has never laid down anything of value. His promise, however, would almost reconcile anyone to a war with Japan."

President Theodore Roosevelt sided with the Japanese, condemning the school board's action as "a wicked absurdity." There was little he could do, however, because the Supreme Court had declared school segregation legal eleven years earlier. To avoid a possible war with Japan, the President made a compromise with the board. It dropped its segregation proposal and he in turn issued an executive order prohibiting further immigration of Japanese workers. Afterwards the United States and Japan worked out an arrangement, the Gentlemen's Agreement of 1908, whereby the Japanese Government refused to issue passports to laborers who wanted to move to the United States. This gave the Japanese a way to save face and cooperate with American demands at the same time. After 1908 Japanese immigration dropped to under two thousand a year, less than the number who returned home annually. Once laborers were barred, almost all the Japanese immigrants were women.

As in the Chinese-American community, men outnumbered women in Little Tokyo three to one, forcing many bachelors to look to the Orient for wives. Since they did not have the money to travel home, they resorted to the exchange of photographs, a method also used by some eastern European immigrants to find brides. Japanese did not import their women as fiancées, however: they married them first by proxy in Japan. Proxy weddings were not repugnant to the Japanese, whose marriages were arranged by parents in any case, but some Californians took exception to the practice. A few disapproved of it as a bizarre custom, but more were afraid that the Japanese-American population would grow too large and threaten the United States with an internal "Yellow Peril." Once again Californians pressured the Government into excluding Orientals—this time female—and once again Japan voluntarily cooperated. In 1921 the two governments concluded the so-called Ladies Agreement ending the importation of "picture brides." Then, only three years later, Congress passed the Johnson-Reed Act, which denied Orientals even a face-saving token quota. In an official letter the Japanese government protested: "The patient, loyal, and scrupulous observances for more than sixteen years, of these self-denying regulations . . . now seems to be wasted."

Prejudice against the Japanese did not die with the Johnson-Reed Act. For seventeen years it festered below the surface, until, triggered by the Japanese attack on Pearl Harbor, it exploded with unprecedented fury.

AMERICA'S CONCENTRATION CAMPS

As losses in the Pacific mounted during World War II, American morale dipped and suspicion of Japanese-Americans spread. People began to fear that a fifth column was forming on the West Coast. California's Attorney General, Earl Warren, called the "Japanese situation" the most vulnerable point in the entire civilian defense effort. Even the fact that no sabotage had occurred was viewed with alarm. Veteran political analyst Walter Lippmann predicted, "It is a sign that the blow is well organized and that it is held back until it can be struck with maximum effect." General John L. De Witt, who was in charge of the Western Defense Command, asserted:

I don't want any of them [persons of Japanese ancestry] here. They are a dangerous element. . . . It makes no difference whether he is an American citizen, he is still a Japanese. You needn't worry about the Italians at all except in certain cases. Also the same for the Germans except in individual cases. But we must worry about the Japanese all the time until he is wiped off the map.

Although the F.B.I. and the Navy did not see the need for such a move, the War Department evacuated all Japanese living in the three West Coast states on General De Witt's insistence. In Hawaii, where 160,000 Americans of Japanese ancestry lived two thousand miles closer to the enemy no such removal was deemed necessary. Nevertheless, the evacuation order was signed by President Franklin D. Roosevelt, endorsed by both houses of Congress, and upheld by the Supreme Court.

Over one hundred and ten thousand Japanese, two-thirds of them American citizens, were forced to abandon their homes. In many instances people were given less than forty-eight hours to pack their belongings and move out with their children. Some families had to leave crops standing in the fields, others had to sell businesses for a fraction of their worth. After a short stay in temporary camps the Japanese were sent to ten hastily constructed relocation centers in isolated parts of the country. Here many sat out the war behind barbed wire fences. In almost all the centers, the internees were crowded into inadequate shelters with no indoor plumbing and, in the frigid camps of Wyoming and Idaho, only antique potbellied stoves for heat.

The wartime evacuation of the Japanese marked a radical departure for the United States Government. For the first time it had declared group affiliation rather than individual guilt a legitimate cause for indictment. On that premise it proceeded to arrest and convict the Japanese without trial, clearly denying them their legal rights. The Government's action was all the more shocking in view of the fact that not even one proven case of sabotage or spying was uncovered among Japanese-Americans. Since no other enemy aliens, much less American citizens, were ever singled out for such discriminatory wartime treatment, one can only conclude that deep-seated racism was at the heart of the matter. During the post-war era the Japanese were successful in obtaining $200,000,000 from the government or slightly over a third of their property losses. But these reparations do not absolve the country from guilt.

It would have been understandable for the Japanese to react to evacuation with bitterness, and some five thousand did renounce their American citizenship, although most later reclaimed it. The vast majority of Japanese, however, decided on a policy of "realistic resignation." Members of the Japanese-American Citizens League (JACL) set the pattern of positive action by helping to prepare the relocation centers. Later thousands of Nisei showed their loyalty to America by picking a bumper crop of sugar beets that were going to rot for lack of harvesters.

After Pearl Harbor the JACL repeatedly petitioned the Government to allow Nisei to join the Armed Forces. Then in 1943 the Army formed an experimental all-Nisei combat unit to fight in Italy. It proved so successful that eventually some twenty-six thousand Japanese-Americans—half from Hawaii and half

During World War II, Americans of Japanese
ancestry, most of them citizens, were forced to
abandon their homes, farms and businesses
and move to isolated relocation centers.
WAR RELOCATION AUTHORITY

from the mainland—served in the Armed Forces. The Nisei's segregated unit, the 442nd Regimental Combat Team (including the 100th Infantry Battalion) lived up to its motto "Go for broke." According to General Mark Clark, the 442nd was the most decorated unit in the entire military history of the United States. In addition to the men who fought in Europe, over six thousand Nisei also served in the Pacific, a well-kept secret until V-J Day. At one point on the India-Burma front a Nisei passed himself off as a Japanese officer. He ordered sixteen Japanese to stack their arms and then he marched them off to American territory using commands he had learned as a visiting student in Tokyo.

❧ INTO AMERICAN LIFE

World War II marked a turning point in the lives of the Chinese and Japanese in America. Before that time the second generation had achieved among the highest educational levels of any minority—higher than that of the natives as a whole—but they had found all doors locked to them. Chinese and Japanese Phi Beta Kappa scholars could be found doing "field work" in their fathers' curio shops and fruit stands because they could not find more suitable employment. In 1928 the Stanford University placement service declared:

It is almost impossible to place a Chinese or Japanese of either the first or second generation in any kind of position, engineering, manufacturing or business. Many firms have general regulations against employing them; others object to them on the grounds that the other men employed by the firms do not care to work with them.

Then after Pearl Harbor, China became our ally and American policy underwent a change. In accordance with our new relationship as comrades-in-arms, the United States made the symbolic gesture of repealing Chinese exclusion and establishing in its stead a token immigration quota of 105. At the same time white employers took Chinese-Americans into jobs they would not have considered them for previously. In 1940 only 3 per cent of the Chinese were professionals, but by 1960 a full 18 per cent were in that class. The Japanese, too, found many new opportunities available to them after the war. Their outstanding record in battle, American contrition over relocation and, in some instances, a change of residence away from the West Coast ushered in the new era. Significantly only five Nisei were in Federal Civil Service jobs before the war but within ten years of V-J Day over ten thousand held Government positions. Thousands more went into white collar jobs in other fields. Then, in 1952, with the McCarran-Walter Act, the United States took the long-overdue step of ending its ban on the naturalization of Oriental immigrants. At last, the Chinese and Japanese were released from their second-class status in American law and accorded the same rights as European newcomers.

Before World War II the Orientals had clustered together in Chinatowns and Little Tokyos, enclaves far more self-sufficient than the ghettos of eastern European immigrants. In addition to the standard shops and services, the Chinese and Japanese had established their own savings and loan associations, informal courts, welfare societies, chambers of commerce, town halls and places of worship. Like other immigrants, they had formed clubs to compensate for their exclusion from American life. And since they were more rigidly segregated than Europeans, they had even more of these ethnic societies. Indeed, a survey conducted in 1939 counted four hundred and eighty-six Nisei organizations active on the West Coast. After World War II many Orientals took advantage of America's new attitude to move away from their crowded enclaves, and with the physical move came an inevitable weakening of ties. Today, while they may still return to Chinatown or Little Tokyo to shop and dine, their lives no longer revolve around ghetto institutions.

When the Orientals moved out of their enclaves they experienced the same "generation gap" as European immigrants. In their desire to be like other Americans, most young Orientals broke away from their parents' traditional beliefs, Buddhism, Shintoism and Confucianism, and joined a Christian church. The second and third generations also rebelled against studying their ancestral languages and deprecated their parents' customs as "old-fashioned." In the past both the Chinese and Japanese prided themselves on an almost nonexistent crime record. But as their children have been exposed more and more to the same forces as other American youngsters, there has been some juvenile delinquency among them. In most cases, however, family life continues to be strong and parents are vigorously trying to combat the delinquency problem.

Until World War II the populations of the Chinese and Japanese communities remained quite static. Then, in 1947, amendments to the "War Brides" and "Fiancées" Acts permitted thousands of Oriental wives and children of American servicemen to immigrate. Fifteen years later President Kennedy admitted fifteen thousand refugees from Communist China who were living temporarily in Hong Kong and Taiwan. As a result of these rulings and the Immigration Act of 1965, the Chinese-American community has nearly tripled and the Japanese-American population has also grown substantially.

The Chinese refugees have gravitated toward the large Chinatowns of New York, San Francisco, and a few other cities, where they feel most secure. Coming in such great numbers, they have strained the already limited facilities of these enclaves. Housing is scarce in Chinatowns and the newcomers have found, as did earlier arrivals, that they must pay relatively high rents for cramped, shabby quarters. The refugees have also had to start out in the hardest, lowest-paying jobs, but the climb upward will surely be easier for them than it was for their predecessors. Happily, the newest Chinese-Americans will not have to contend with the bitter racial antagonisms that, in the case of Orientals at least, are a thing of the past.

Grant Steet, Chinatown, San Francisco. Because of the increased social mobility enjoyed by Orientals since World War II, Chinatowns and Little Tokyos are no longer closed to American influences. Some enclaves still retain their distinctive appearance, however.
UNION PACIFIC RAILROAD PHOTO

Like Little Italy and Chinatown, *El Barrio* has many
grocery stores that sell produce traditionally used
by local customers. This grocer has stocked many
of the tropical fruits that Puerto Ricans particularly
enjoy. UNITED PRESS INTERNATIONAL PHOTO

Citizen Immigrants

Before the Johnson-Reed act of 1924, immigration from the Americas was overshadowed by the great influx from Europe. Then, with that tide effectively dammed, the arrival of our Western Hemisphere neighbors became both actually and relatively more important. Canada had been trading populations with the United States since 1776, but in the 1920's the current ran strongly in favor of this country. During that decade almost one million Canadians crossed the forty-ninth parallel to take advantage of our booming economy. The small number among them who spoke French gravitated toward established French-Canadian enclaves in New England. But the majority, who were of British ancestry, flocked to the industrial centers of the Middle West, where they scattered amongst the general population. After 1930 the Depression called a halt to Canadian emigration and subsequent industrialization at home prevented it from reviving on a large scale.

More obvious and more enduring than the Canadian movement was the influx from Mexico. After 1900 a surge of railroad-building and the rapid expansion of agriculture created an urgent need for unskilled, migratory labor in the southwest. Lacking a pool of cheap native workers or Orientals, employers and labor contractors began to look for men south of the Rio Grande. The recruiters met with an enthusiastic response and in time Mexicans accounted for 12 per cent of the population of the southwest. At first Mexican-Americans worked almost exclusively in agriculture, cultivating and processing cotton, vegetables, fruit, and sugar cane; but in recent years they have been moving into industrial jobs as well. On the whole, the Mexican-Americans' economic and social advancement has been painfully slow, due in large measure to regional prejudices against them.

At the same time that Mexicans started to migrate in large numbers to the Southwest, West Indians began to establish themselves in cities along the eastern seaboard, especially New York and Boston. Negroes from the British West Indies formed the greatest proportion of the incoming throng, but there were smaller contingents from Cuba, Haiti, Puerto Rico, and the French West Indies as well. Because their backgrounds differed so greatly, the West Indians performed a wider variety of jobs than most immigrant groups. Many were unskilled country people who were equipped to do only the most menial labor in the United States. But others, such as Jamaican and Cuban cigar makers and English-speaking professionals, had been highly trained, and they took up familiar work here. Although most West Indian Negroes improved their financial position by moving to the United States, our rigid color line drastically curtailed their social mobility. In 1952 the McCarran-Walter Act abruptly terminated immigration from the British West Indies. People continued to move up from the Caribbean, however, for by that time the major source of the exodus had shifted from the islands of Jamaica, Trinidad, and Barbados to Puerto Rico, which was not affected by the new law.

◆2 PUERTO RICO

The island of Puerto Rico is just one hundred and nine miles long and thirty-nine miles wide—about half the size of New Jersey. It is lush and mountainous but without developed natural resources. Some years after Columbus discovered the island, Spanish *conquistadores* began to establish sugar plantations there, importing African slaves to do the work. Slavery was finally abolished in 1873 and the ex-slaves were allowed to mingle quite freely with the white population—far more freely, in fact, than their counterparts in the United States. But since the former slaves were without property, skills or education, they remained a poverty-stricken underclass for whom the rulers did little.

In 1898 after four hundred years of Spanish rule, Puerto Rico passed into American hands as a prize of the Spanish-American War. From the people's point of view there was little to distinguish American from Spanish colonialism. The United States did make some improvements in the fields of health and education, but unemployment remained high and poverty continued to be widespread. Only in 1947 when Puerto Rico got the right to elect its own governor and in 1952 when the island attained commonwealth status did the situation really begin to improve. Under the energetic leadership of Governor Luis Muñoz Marín, the islanders set about to diversify and industrialize the economy and improve the quality of their lives. Puerto Ricans called their self-help program "Operation Bootstrap," but the hundreds of private citizens and officials who went to observe it often referred to their effort as "the miracle of the Caribbean." Fifteen hundred new factories were started, directly or indirectly creating almost three hundred thousand jobs. Per capita income rose from $121 in 1940 to $1,000 in 1967, more than twice the average for Latin America. During the same period real living standards rose faster than in any underdeveloped country in the world.

Ironically, efforts to improve conditions in Puerto Rico created some new problems which helped bring about a large-scale flight from the island. When the United States Health Service wiped out malaria and other diseases and improved medical services on the island, the death rate fell to below the mainland figure. Because Puerto Rico's birth rate remained very high, the population doubled between 1900 and 1950, making the island one of the most crowded places in the world. No matter how fast "Operation Bootstrap" created new jobs, the population simply outran them. Unemployment hovered at triple the American rate.

"Operation Bootstrap" ushered in "the revolution of rising aspirations" in Puerto Rico. As the people started to enjoy a modicum of prosperity, they began to desire even greater wealth and more acquisitions. Compared to Latin America their own land might be a paradise, but compared to the mainland it was still a very poor place with limited opportunities for advancement. The United States, the traditional land of opportunity, beckoned the young and ambitious. The great volume of American books, movies, TV shows, and goods that flooded the island reinforced their desire to be off. While, like other immigrants, the Puerto Ricans changed homes basically to increase their earning power, they were also mindful of the superior schools, fine hospitals, and other services the mainland offered. Following in the steps of the southern and eastern Europeans who preceded them, most Puerto Ricans chose to start their new lives in New York.

ℯ NEW YORK

In the early twentieth century Puerto Ricans bound for the mainland had to choose between ships stopping at Gulf Coast ports and those anchoring in New York. Although the islanders found the southern climate more appealing, the fare to New York was cheaper and ships called there more frequently. Moreover, most Puerto Ricans are of mixed Spanish and Negro parentage and many feared that their dark complexions would make them objects of discrimination in the South. For these reasons almost all the emigrants embarked for New York.

At first the city's "pioneer" Puerto Rican community consisted of cigar makers, merchant seamen, factory workers, businessmen, and domestics. In the 1920's their number was swelled by experienced needlewomen who were recruited for the city's garment center. Then, in the twenty years following World War II, New York's Puerto Rican population jumped from seventy thousand to seven hundred thousand. The postwar business boom and corresponding job opportunities attracted the islanders while the inauguration of regular airplane service between San Juan and New York facilitated their coming. In recent years Puerto Ricans have begun to move to a number of mainland cities and suburbs, but over nine hundred and fifty thousand, or about 70 per cent of all the migrants, still live in New York.

Hampered by language difficulties and lack of education or capital, the Puerto Ricans could only take the most menial and lowest-paying jobs in the city. Often those with skills had to accept work below their level of competence because older residents had preempted the better positions. By filling in at the bottom level, however, the Puerto Ricans quickly made themselves invaluable to New York's economic life. They took over jobs in toy and radio assembly lines, food plants, and small jewelry factories. They manned hospital, laundry and building maintenance crews. Many hotel and restaurant owners claimed that if it were not for their Puerto Rican employees they would have had to shut down. And the head of Local 142 of the International Ladies Garment Workers Union averred that "if it hadn't been for the Spanish, the industry would have left New York."

The I.L.G.W.U., the International Union of Electrical Workers, and a few other labor organizations went out of their way to help Puerto Rican workers. They actively recruited the newcomers and provided them with training programs and jobs. Racket unions, too, sought out Puerto Ricans—but with the intention of exploiting rather than helping them. These organizations signed "sweetheart" contracts with unscrupulous employers unionizing their businesses without the workers' knowledge.

In the 1920's expert needleworkers were recruited
in Puerto Rico for New York's clothing industry.
Today Puerto Rican men and women have a
variety of jobs in the garment center.
BROWN BROTHERS

Later the employees discovered they had to pay dues to a union that guaranteed them neither rest periods, raises nor seniority rights. Moreover, they were often laid off just before paid vacations. The racket union swindle came to light in 1956 and the following year the American Federation of Labor ousted the worst offenders from their ranks. Although the A.F. of L.'s stand prevented a repetition of the fraud, the one hundred thousand low-salaried Puerto Rican workers who had been caught in it remained deeply hostile to the whole labor movement. Legitimate unions that either refused to accept Puerto Rican members or were insensitive to their special needs did little to improve labor's tarnished image in the Spanish-speaking community.

The kind of jobs held by Puerto Ricans directly affected how they lived. Since their jobs usually paid the least, they had to take the cheapest dwellings in the city—often the very same tenements which had housed millions of "new" immigrants. In 1890 Jacob Riis vehemently attacked the jerry-built tenements as "scarcely fit to shelter brutes." What would he have said in 1950, after more than half a century of landlord neglect and tenant abuse? Over the years wiring had gone bad, water pipes had burst, roofs had sprung leaks, and furnaces had stopped giving heat. As Piri Thomas, a graduate of Spanish Harlem, describes latter-day tenement-dwelling in his autobiography, *Down These Mean Streets:*

In the summer the cooped-up apartments in Harlem seem to catch all the heat and improve on it. It's the same in the winter. The cold, plastered walls embrace the cold from outside and make it a part of the apartment, till you don't know whether it's better to freeze out in the snow or by the stove, where four jets, wide open, spout futile, blue-yellow flames. It's hard on the rats, too.

Despite their advanced state of decay, tenements became more in demand than ever after World War II as waves of Puerto Ricans and southern Negroes moved up to New York. The housing shortage grew so acute that people bribed landlords and superintendents for the privilege of living in miserable hovels. In 1954 a survey of poor Spanish Harlem residents revealed that one hundred and nineteen people had paid a total of $61,000 in "bonuses" for their slum apartments! Many slumlords milked their properties by throwing up flimsy interior partitions and charging almost the same rents for single rooms as they had for whole apartments. This partitioning was a particular hardship for Puerto Rican families which usually included several children. Newcomers who held good jobs were also frustrated in their attempts to find a decent place to live. Although they could afford something better, they were often trapped in the slums by discrimination. Or, if they did succeed in obtaining an apartment in a better building, the owner usually assumed that the property would start to deteriorate so he cut services—which assured that it did.

The Puerto Ricans arrived in New York in great numbers just as the city was embarking upon a massive program of urban redevelopment. On block after block high-rise apartment houses began to replace rundown tenements. While some islanders did obtain homes in these projects, many others found that the city maintained strict entrance requirements—requirements they could not meet. And those people who lost their homes to a project were not necessarily guaranteed a place in the low-income, low-rent buildings. To be sure, New York City assumed responsibility for the displaced, but some poor people were shuttled from condemned tenement to condemned tenement until the city found them a permanent place to live. Even many people who qualified for public projects often had to scramble around for interim housing until a city-owned apartment became available to them. Over the years the number of applicants rapidly outstripped vacancies until by 1964 there were eighty-five thousand applicants for six thousand.availabilities. Five years later the waiting list had grown to one hundred and eighty-nine thousand while the number of availabilities had increased only slightly. At the going rate of construction the last people on the list would move into a public housing project in fifty-one years!

The Puerto Ricans' housing plight—which shows no signs of improving—is distressing in itself, but it becomes even more tragic when considered in the context of American opportunity. As the President's Committee on Urban Housing noted in 1968:

The place a man lives is more than just another commodity, service or possession. It is a symbol of his status, an extension of his personality, a part of his identity, a determinant of many of the benefits— and disadvantages—of society that will come to him and his family: schooling, police protection, municipal services, neighborhood environment, access (or lack of access) to a hundred possibilities of life and culture.

EL BARRIO

The most striking contrast between the rich and the poor areas of Manhattan is in the visible wealth of the one and the visible children of the other. Also, there is the obvious restraint of the one and the expressiveness of the other. In East Harlem, music is everywhere, and visible gaiety, anger, fear, love, hatred.

—*Spanish Harlem*
Patricia Cayo Sexton

Puerto Rican children often must find recreation in the city's streets and back alleys. Here, some boys and girls are playing among the trash in one of *El Barrio's* empty lots. ARTHUR TRESS

East Harlem, the oldest and best-known Puerto Rican settlement on the mainland, occupies roughly one square mile in the northeast corner of Manhattan Island. Originally an area of tranquil farms, East Harlem became the home of Irish and German immigrants in the second half of the nineteenth century. A few decades later great numbers of Italians and Jews started to move into the area and whole blocks of tenements were built to accommodate them. When the "new" immigrants began moving out to better quarters in the 1920's, Puerto Ricans, Cubans, and Dominicans came in to take up their vacant apartments. Indeed, so many Latin Americans gravitated to the area that it became known as "Spanish Harlem." To Puerto Ricans it is simply *El Barrio,* "the neighborhood."

Today, despite the impersonality of its giant housing projects, *El Barrio* still retains much of its community flavor. Many of the store signs, conversations, and newsstand publications are in Spanish and lively Puerto Rican music emanates from a thousand transistor radios. East Harlem's travel agencies feature flights to "La Isla Encantada" and grocery stores prominently display Puerto Rican specialities. Since *El Barrio* offers little in the way of vestpocket parks, the islanders, who are accustomed to gathering in plazas, do their socializing on the street. At all hours of the day men congregate in small knots to talk or play cards and dominoes while women sit on tenement stoops taking a respite from their housework. Children use the pavement as a playground. In the summer months, especially, the streets of Spanish Harlem fairly burst with humanity. As Piri Thomas describes the scene:

All the blocks are alive, like many-legged cats crawling with fleas. People are all over the place. Stoops are occupied like bleacher sections at a game, and beer flows like there's nothing else to drink. The block musicians pound out gone beats on tin cans and conga drums and bongos. And kids are playing all over the place—on fire escapes, under cars, in alleys, back yards, hallways.

El Barrio's religious life is almost as diverse as its street scene. One cannot walk very far in the area without encountering a Catholic church, a Pentecostal house of worship or a "drugstore" selling Spiritualistic cures. Eighty-five per cent of the migrants are Catholic, but their ties to the Church in Puerto Rico are often tenuous and many people stop attending mass altogether after moving to the mainland. For a number of years the Catholic Church has been trying to counteract this phenomenon by importing or training Spanish-speaking priests, holding certain masses in Spanish, and offering the newcomers a variety of social services. So far these efforts have met with mixed results.

At the same time that the Catholic Church has been trying to hold on to its Puerto Rican members, a great number of other churches in New York—estimated at two hundred in the mid-1950's—have been attempting to convert them to Protestantism. Today, the East Harlem Protestant Parish is the most active of the Protestant groups in *El Barrio*. Through its work with dope addicts, troubled teenagers and community action groups it reaches a few thousand people yearly. Yet despite the community's enthusiastic response to its social activities and self-help programs, the Parish has not effected a great number of conversions.

Far more popular with Puerto Ricans than the traditional Protestant denominations are those evangelical sects which usually call themselves Pentecostals. These groups are characterized by an emotional, joyful worship of God and a warm fellowship among members which alienated migrants find tremendously appealing. While a few Pentecostal churches are quite large, most have only one hundred to one hundred and fifty members and meet in small stores or abandoned Jewish synagogues. Pentecostal revival meetings take place every night of the week in *El Barrio*. They are lively affairs in which ritual and personal testimony are interspersed with hymns sung to the accompaniment of tambourines, guitars, and handclapping.

Many people who belong to Catholic and Protestant churches also practice Spiritualism. They gather in private apartments to enact mystical rites whose significance is apparent only to the initiated. Since these rituals are rarely performed publicly, it is impossible to know how many people are involved. The *Jardines Botánicas* that sell the cult's herbs, oils, and mystical books, however, can sometimes be found two to a block in Spanish Harlem.

In addition to being involved in religious organizations, many Puerto Ricans participate in "hometown" clubs, fraternal orders, professional associations, and businessmen's clubs. Almost all of these groups take part in the Puerto Rican Day parade which in 1969 consisted of seventy-five thousand marchers. But this overwhelming turnout notwithstanding, most Puerto Rican organizations are merely small social clubs without the authority that similar immigrant groups wielded over their members.

Although large housing projects have depersonalized Spanish Harlem to some extent, there are still many signs of Puerto Rican culture in *El Barrio*. Here, a neighborhood store offers religious articles, herbs and incense.

Nor is Spanish Harlem interlaced with the network of private hospitals, social agencies, savings and loan associations, and insurance companies that were started and supported by earlier immigrant groups. Even New York's Spanish-language press and radio and television stations are owned by non-Puerto Ricans. That the newcomers have not gone further in establishing a traditional immigrant community can be attributed in part to their constant relocation within New York and frequent trips back to Puerto Rico. Even more important, the government now provides so many public services that voluntary associations would merely duplicate its work.

Instead of building a conventional ethnic community, the Puerto Ricans are organizing themselves into a pressure bloc. They are more interested in obtaining equal opportunities than they are in perpetuating a distinctive cultural heritage. In the last few years the islanders have formed a number of powerful groups in New York, including the Puerto Rican Community Development Project and the Citywide Puerto Rican Action Movement. Young people, who seem to believe more strongly than their elders in social change, are often in the vanguard of the civil rights protests. In 1969 a number of young Puerto Ricans demonstrated effectively with blacks to get increased minority representation in the student body of New York's City University.

It is ironical and not a little sad that Puerto Ricans find themselves battling Negroes for control of antipoverty programs. The islanders learned their political tactics from the blacks and share with them the goals of the civil rights movement. Yet, in a typical case, planning for Harlem's Millbank-

Frawley Circle urban renewal area was snarled for years and finally came to a halt because of a power struggle between the two groups. Even without the question of community control, however, there would be conflict between the newcomers and the blacks. For one thing, they compete for the same jobs. For another, some Puerto Ricans resent being classified with black Americans while many blacks feel that the Puerto Ricans, as "whites," harbor prejudices against them. Although not always apparent, many of the tensions in East Harlem today can be traced to differences in race and ethnic affiliation.

As the newest and poorest additions to New York City, the Puerto Ricans are susceptible to crime, dope addiction, broken families, and mental and physical breakdowns. And, to be sure, these problems are very much in evidence in *El Barrio*. But side by side with the misery are the warmth and color that have always been the strength of the ghetto.

COMMUTING

Some earlier immigrant groups had a high rate of return to the Old Country. But none produced anything like the heavy two-way traffic that flows constantly between Puerto Rico and the mainland. Indeed, so many Puerto Ricans fly back each year that island politicians now campaign for votes in New York. To earlier immigrants a trip home meant that a man had either struck it rich or failed miserably in the States. But today the journey from New York to San Juan is so fast, cheap and commonplace that the migrants attach no such special significance to it.

While many Puerto Ricans fly home just for a visit, thousands more return with the intention of staying on. Usually they are motivated by the same factor that caused them to leave the island in the first place: economic betterment. The ongoing "Operation Bootstrap" with its myriad job opportunities provides the big attraction. And the migrants, armed with mainland skills, education and proficiency in English, can compete very favorably for many of these places. Indeed, between 1955 and 1960 twenty-eight per cent of the professional openings and thirty-six per cent of the new manufacturing and merchandising jobs were filled by returnees. Often, a downturn in the mainland business cycle sparks the decision to go home; every recession in recent years has been followed by an increased movement to the island. In addition to economic considerations, crowded subways, dangerous streets and the heavy burden of being a Puerto Rican in the States cause many to return home.

When the migrants land in San Juan their sense of relief is immediate. No icy winds sting their faces, no black soot dirties their clothes. They are reunited with their parents, speak Spanish freely and no longer have to apologize to anyone for their origins. Yet in many cases the elation wears off quickly. The migrants hear so many inflated stories about Puerto Rico's booming economy that they return home without definite plans, confident that they will find work somewhere. Good jobs are increasingly hard to come by, however. Cuban refugees, Latin American immigrants, and Puerto Rico's own workers create stiff competition for every opening. Moreover, even when the returnees do find employment, their salaries are apt to be lower than they were in the States, while the cost of living is almost as high.

Since the most typical returnees are married couples in their thirties and forties, a great number of children are also involved in the reverse migration. The young people, who are more "Americanized" than their parents, find the move a great wrench in their lives. Generally, they cannot read or write Spanish and their speaking vocabulary is limited to household words. This puts them at a distinct disadvantage in Puerto Rican schools where instruction is given exclusively in Spanish. The social adjustment is hardest for teenagers who have lived on the mainland all their lives. They call themselves "New York Puerto Ricans" and speak Spanish with an English accent. One of their number, nineteen-year-old Rudy Marrero, was quoted in *The New York Times* magazine on the conflict between the young returnees and the "Puerto Rican Puerto Ricans":

We are disliked because we talk in English. They like to take their liquor by putting the bottle to their mouths; we like to drink it slowly. They dance hick style; we dance Palladium style. I think the Puerto Rican kids are jealous of us. And they think that all of us from New York are tough gang hoods.

There are now over half a million people in Puerto Rico who have lived in the States for a year or more and their influence is enormous. Returnees are contributing much-needed skills and expertise to the island's economy and, through the stores and factories they open, they are also creating new jobs for other Puerto Ricans. Moreover, since so many of them want to purchase their own homes, they are giving the construction industry a boost. But the reverse migration is also posing severe problems for Puerto Rico. Caught unawares by the great volume of returnees in the early 1960's, government planners had not provided for adequate public facilities or services. As a result, the school system is now terribly overburdened and over a third of the children attend classes for only half a day.

The reverse migration is also having far-reaching effects on the quality of life on the island. Returnees are bringing back with them the American drive for wealth and status. They are introducing American modes of recreation, dress, and entertainment. And they are "corrupting" the Spanish language with many English words and some made-up adaptations. Many enlightened Puerto Ricans fear that in the not-too-distant future Americanization could obliterate Puerto Rico's cultural identity. To prevent this from happening, the government launched "Operation Serenity," an educational program emphasizing the island's spiritual values and Spanish antecedents.

Even as "commuting" is Americanizing life in Puerto Rico, it is helping to delay the islanders' assimilation on the mainland. Their on-going contact with Latin culture has led some observers to predict that Puerto Ricans will never shed their ethnic distinctiveness. "Puerto Ricans won't disappear into the American melting pot as early immigrants did," declared psychologist Joshua A. Fishman in 1968. But other evidence would seem to dispute Dr. Fishman's prognosis. In the past, minority life styles have always yielded to the majority. This standardization process can be seen today in the eradication of sectional differences in the United States. Moreover, second and third generation Puerto Rican migrants already identify more with the culture of their "American" peers than with that of their parents. They do not share the first generation's dream of returning to Puerto Rico. As mainland-bred Bob Ortiz commented, "When I first saw Puerto Rico it was a culture shock. It was so very rural. To me it's not an enchanted island." And their increased interest in civil rights and community improvement shows conclusively that young Puerto Ricans feel that their future is here—as full, unhyphenated citizens. When asked why he attends neighborhood action meetings on 103rd Street in *El Barrio*, fourteen-year-old George Vega replied, "This block is my home; I know nothing else."

NEWCOMERS: YESTERDAY AND TODAY

In many ways it is easier for Puerto Ricans to migrate than it was for earlier immigrant groups. Ever since 1899, when they were granted the right of free access to the States, the islanders have been able to move here without the health inspections and quota restrictions that plagued other aspiring entrants. They also enjoy a far pleasanter journey. Compared to the Europeans' or Orientals' long confinement aboard ship, the Puerto Ricans' three-hour plane trip seems like a ride on a magic carpet. Psychologically, too, the Puerto Ricans have an advantage over their forerunners. Through the Commonwealth's close association with the United States, they are familiar with many American institutions even before they leave home.

Yet despite their American citizenship, the islanders are still "strangers in a strange land" when they arrive in New

York. They are more urbanized than immigrants of years past, but their experience with Puerto Rico's tranquil cities has left them essentially unprepared for the towering skyscrapers, nerve-shattering noise and wall-to-wall humanity that is Manhattan Island. On top of this, the newcomers cannot communicate effectively in English, a language they speak haltingly or not at all. And, their exposure to American life via movies and TV notwithstanding, at close range they often find mainland customs, food, music, and dress very unfamiliar. Contact with residents does little to overcome their sense of alienation, because New Yorkers generally greet strangers with an indifference almost indistinguishable from hostility.

Earlier arrivals could gradually become acclimated to American life by surrounding themselves with thousands of fellow countrymen. But New York's desperate housing shortage and slum clearance program no longer permit the large, homogeneous neighborhoods of years past. Indeed, due to the bulldozer, even Spanish Harlem is only 40 per cent "Spanish" today. Puerto Ricans must scatter to all parts of the city, taking up residence wherever they can find vacant apartments. While the islanders do not generally share tenement buildings with other groups, they are likely to live next door to them. And public housing projects, where 15 per cent of the migrants live, are well integrated.

Without large ghettos acting as a buffer, Puerto Ricans discover culture conflicts faster than other groups. It does not take migrant children long to realize, for example, that their American playmates are allowed to walk to school unescorted and the little newcomers quickly demand the same privilege.

Teenage girls, whose dates must be chaperoned on the island, are ridiculed by their American peers for following such an "old-fashioned" custom here. They, too, rebel. But far more serious than either of these problems is the clash between Puerto Rico's patriarchal family system and our more democratic one. In Puerto Rico the man is the undisputed head of the family, but in the States women participate fully in decision-making. Latin men are usually their families' sole support, but American women are often wage-earners too. After living on the mainland for a while and taking jobs themselves, the normally self-effacing Puerto Rican women become almost as assertive as their American counterparts. Many Puerto Rican men resent their wives' new independence, complaining that in America women are "spoiled." The tensions which result from this conflict strain some marriages to the breaking point.

Because Puerto Ricans are migrating in an era of government enlightenment, they have services at their disposal which no other group enjoyed. The Commonwealth's Migration Division and the United States Employment Service work in close cooperation to help the newcomers obtain job training and placement. Their help frees the islanders from dependence on grasping padrones, political bosses—or pot luck. New York City does its share by providing aid to dependent children and supplemental incomes for men without jobs or with very low-paying ones. This assistance is a great boon to newcomers who have no reserves to fall back on while trying to get established here. Because of welfare, Puerto Ricans are relieved of some of the anxieties that plagued earlier poor immigrants.

But timing, which is helping them in so many ways, is

working against them in the labor market. Today's complex society demands more technical expertise than ever before. And while the Puerto Ricans are more highly skilled and better-educated than most of our immigrant ancestors, they are far behind native workers in both respects. Moreover, their migration has coincided with the automation of countless unskilled and semiskilled jobs, traditional starting points for all newcomers. With the better positions beyond their grasp and the blue collar jobs fast disappearing, Puerto Ricans often find themselves without any work at all. Not surprisingly, their unemployment rate is more than double that of other Americans.

Another serious problem for Puerto Ricans that European newcomers did not have to face is the color bar. Many Americans consider the islanders "colored" and discriminate accordingly. Prejudice is not unknown in Puerto Rico, where the upper and middle classes are almost entirely white. However, discrimination there is based more on economic status than race and people socialize and marry without regard to skin color. It comes as quite a shock to Puerto Rican migrants, then, when they are confronted with blatant racial prejudice in the States. Some light-skinned people try to escape its sting by severing all relations with the group. Some of the darker newcomers go to the opposite extreme and cling fiercely to the Spanish language lest they be classified as Negro. At one time there was some speculation that the Puerto Rican community would split along color lines, but this never occurred. Instead, with increased civil rights activity, the group is more solidified than ever before.

In the twenty-five years since their migration began in earnest, the Puerto Ricans have established an impressive record of achievement on the mainland—one which compares favorably with that of other newcomers at a similar stage of development. Despite a constantly shifting clientele and competition from chain stores, Puerto Ricans now own more than ten thousand businesses in New York City. Despite an unfavorable job market they have more earning power than immigrants of fifty years ago. And despite difficulties with the language, thirty-eight thousand first and second generation Puerto Rican Americans have graduated from high school in New York state with a number of them going on to college and graduate school. But beyond all that, Puerto Ricans are helping to break down color barriers through protest and by example. In the long run this may prove to be their biggest achievement of all.

After the "separate but equal" doctrine was pro-
pounded by the Supreme Court in 1896, "Jim Crow"
laws proliferated throughout the South. This was a
sign at a railroad station in Jackson, Mississippi
in 1962. UNITED PRESS INTERNATIONAL PHOTO

Familiar Strangers

BLACK MEN SET FOOT ON AMERICAN soil in 1619, one year before the Pilgrims landed at Plymouth Rock. By normal standards, that early arrival date should have made Negroes the most Americanized of Americans. And if one looks only at their lack of allegiance to other countries or cultures, then, indeed, they are completely assimilated. But if one takes economic advancement and social acceptance as his criteria, then Negroes must be considered as unassimilated as our most recent arrivals. The fact that Negroes have been left out of the American Dream is not merely of academic interest; it presents the most urgent and difficult problem facing the country today. As President Johnson's Commission on Civil Disorders warned, "Our nation is moving toward two societies, one black, one white—separate and unequal." To understand

how the United States arrived at this juncture one must go all
the way back to slave days, when some men owned other men.

❧ THE PECULIAR INSTITUTION

Unlike every other group who came to America, Africans were
not immigrants. They did not leave home of their own free will
and they were not given a chance to advance themselves here.*
Even British convicts, who were also transported to the colonies
involuntarily, could obtain their freedom by working at hard
labor for seven years. But black men, captured on the continent
of Africa and shipped to the New World in chains would remain bound with their children in perpetuity no matter how
long or how diligently they worked.

It was obvious even in the eighteenth century that slavery
directly contradicted the American ideal of democracy. "How
is it that we hear the loudest *yelps* for liberty among the drivers
of Negroes?" asked Dr. Samuel Johnson of London. "How, indeed," agreed many Americans and after the Revolution each
of the northern states set about abolishing slavery. But the introduction of the cotton gin and subsequent expansion of the plantation system made white southerners cling even more tightly
to "the peculiar institution." They passed law upon law to deny
slaves any and all human rights, especially the right to quit. But
then even the Constitution of the United States considered slaves
pieces of property. And so they were treated.

* See first chapter for a discussion of white servitude, the slave trade and
the evolution of slavery on American soil.

Advertisement for the sale of newly-arrived Africans. Because of the tremendous demand for slaves, ship captains could charge—and get—very high prices for their human cargoes.

TO BE SOLD on board the Ship *Bance-Island*, on tuesday the 6th of *May* next, at *Ashley-Ferry*; a choice cargo of about 250 fine healthy

NEGROES, just arrived from the Windward & Rice Coast.
—The utmost care has already been taken, and shall be continued, to keep them free from the least danger of being infected with the SMALL-POX, no boat having been on board, and all other communication with people from *Charles-Town* prevented.

Austin, Laurens, & Appleby.

N. B. Full one Half of the above Negroes have had the SMALL-POX in their own Country.

Some slaves worked at trades or cleaned the master's house and minded his children, but the vast majority tilled the fields, usually in the backbreaking task of growing cotton. To one slave, at least, those fields seemed to stretch "from one end of the earth to the other." The slaves tended the cotton for twelve hours or more, with only a short break for lunch. Then they returned to their quarters to chop wood, feed the mules and do other chores. After a small supper they fell into bed, ready to be on their feet at four or five the next morning. Children were gradually broken into this harsh routine from the age of six, so that by the time they were ten they were holding down regular work assignments.

While immigrants in the North also endured long hours, exhausting drudgery and slum apartments little better than the slaves' shacks, their lot was still incomparably better. They were free and they got paid. Moreover, while the newcomers could be fired, laid off or blackballed, they were protected by law from physical harassment. But slaves enjoyed no such legal protection, so masters could and did mete out corporal punishment with impunity. Sometimes the white men administered floggings for nothing more serious than "impudence," of which the famous abolitionist Frederick Douglass once wrote:

Impudence [might mean] almost anything, or nothing at all, just according to the caprice of the master or overseer, at the moment. . . . This offense may be committed in various ways: in the tone of an answer; in answering at all; in not answering; in the expression of countenance; in the motion of the head; in the gait, manner and bearing of the slave.

Few slaves went through life without ever suffering corporal punishment. While the law protected immigrants from physical harassment by employers, it did not shield slaves from the ire of their masters. LIBRARY OF CONGRESS

But then impudence was considered far more dangerous in a slave than in a paid employee. For, as well as being a system of economic exploitation, slavery was also a social institution. It was a patriarchy in which white men played the role of omnipotent fathers, and black men took the part of their dependent children. Slaves could not leave the plantation without a pass from the master. Slaves could not meet in groups without a white man present. Slaves could not be taught to read and write lest they become "uppity." And without economic or legal rights, male slaves could not even control their own family life. Having thoroughly debased slaves this way, it was then very easy (not to mention self-gratifying) for white southerners to assume that they were inherently superior to Negroes. This white racism was the most tragic legacy of slavery. Today, more than one hundred years after Emancipation, it is still at the root of America's "Negro problem."

Yet black men did not accept bondage with equanimity. In fact, before the Civil War some two hundred and fifty groups of slaves revolted and in the most famous uprising, the Nat Turner Rebellion, they killed sixty white people. Thousands of other slaves ran away. In the nineteenth century many of them traveled north via the Underground Railroad, an escape route manned by free Negroes and sympathetic whites. But both rebellion and escape entailed considerable risk, a risk that most slaves were not psychologically prepared to take. So, although bitterly resentful, the great majority did the practical thing and stayed on their plantations. They did protest from time to time, however, by breaking equipment, staging slow-

God bless you massa! you feed and clothe us. When we are sick you nurse us. and when too old to work, you provide for us!

These poor creatures are a sacred legacy from my ancestors and while a dollar is left me, nothing shall be spared to increase their comfort and happiness.

The myth of the kind, paternal master and the grateful, happy slave was perpetuated for many years after Emancipation by white Southerners who wanted to keep the Negro "in his place."
THE SMITHSONIAN INSTITUTION

down and sitdown strikes, lying to their masters, and "taking" things from them.

That the slaves were deeply unhappy is quite evident from their spirituals or "sorrow songs." These ballads usually describe life in terms of discouragement and sadness while they speak of death in terms of exaltation. "Nobody Knows the Trouble I've Seen," "Why Don't You Give Up the World," "My Father, How Long?" and "We'll Soon Be Free, the Lord Will Call Us Home" are typical of this genre. When they could, slaves slipped away to quiet arbors to sing out their troubles to God.

❧ RECONSTRUCTION

I looked at my hands to see if I was the same person now I was free. Dere was such a glory over everything, de sun comes like gold through the trees . . .

—Harriet Tubman, runaway slave

After Lee surrendered at Appomattox Court House, Harriet Tubman's reaction was duplicated by blacks all over the South. The emancipated slaves deserted their plantations en masse, taking to the roads to see how freedom felt. For the first time they could enjoy last names, liquor, political meetings, and getting married—for real. Some former slaves exercised their new-found rights by doing nothing at all. Others threw themselves into the task of learning, using the Bible for a text. Their attempts at education were aided by the Freedmen's Bureau and several church organizations, which set up schools and imported Northern teachers. By 1870 these organizations

A classroom scene in Vicksburg, Mississippi.
During Reconstruction former slaves flocked to
Freedmen's schools where they were taught to read
and write for the first time. LIBRARY OF CONGRESS

counted one hundred and fifty thousand blacks studying in their classrooms. During this era, moreover, thirty-three colleges and universities were founded in the South, among them today's leading Negro institutions of higher learning.

The newly freed men took as great an interest in politics as in education. During Reconstruction, that ten-year period when Union troops still occupied parts of the South, seven hundred thousand blacks registered and voted. With their new political power Negroes helped put members of their own race into office. For the first time in America, blacks served as superintendents of education, state treasurers, adjutant generals, judges, and ranking officers of state militia. Robert H. Wood was Mayor of Natchez, Mississippi, and P.B.S. Pinchback held office briefly as Governor of Louisiana. In all, twenty Negroes served in the House of Representatives and two sat in the Senate. Many more were elected to state legislatures and constitutional conventions. While some black politicians were illiterate ex-slaves who were unequal to their offices, others were well-educated, free-born men who performed their duties admirably. They helped draft many competent state laws which included such forward-looking provisions as greater rights for women, penal and judicial reform, and the inauguration of state-supported public schools for both whites and blacks.

But while politics fed the black man's pride, it could not fill his stomach. And, as the months went by, his economic plight grew more and more desperate. Congressmen spent long hours debating what to *do* with the freed man, but their solutions were all political. They passed amendments to the Constitution guaranteeing the Negro freedom, citizenship, and the right to vote.

They made no laws, however, which guaranteed him the right to earn a decent living. Thaddeus Stevens, the Radical Republican, begged his colleagues in the House of Representatives to grant each ex-slave "forty acres and a mule." But that magical phrase, instead of becoming the touchstone of progress, lingered on in history as a melancholy symbol of the Negro's dashed hopes. For shortly after the war, President Andrew Johnson returned confiscated Confederate lands to their former owners instead of distributing them among the ex-slaves. Without that land, the four million freed men were thrown back upon the mercies of their former masters.

But the Civil War had devastated white southern farmers, so that they had no cash with which to pay hired help. It remained for northern capital to bring southern land and labor together in the system known as sharecropping. Under this arrangement, northern bankers lent the farmers the money to get back on their feet again. The farmers then purchased food, tools, seed, equipment, and animals which they, in turn, sold to their Negro tenants or sharecroppers on credit. Theoretically, the tenants should have come out ahead at the end of the season. But in reality the farmers had charged them such exorbitant prices for necessities and rent that their share of the crop could not cover expenses. Thus, the tenants were usually more in debt after harvest than before. Since they had to try to pay off their debt by making a new crop for the same man, sharecropping ultimately reduced many blacks to the status of peons, perpetual debtors little better off than slaves.

This time the North did not come to the Negroes' rescue. As Reconstruction dragged on, many northerners became bored by the eternal "southern question." They wanted to reunite the nation and get on with business as usual. Even onetime liberals started to look the other way when Negro schools were burned down and black men were lynched. Eleven years after the Civil War public opinion supported the withdrawal of troops from the South. Therefore, the nation went along with the political deal that solved the disputed election of 1876 by sending Rutherford B. Hayes to the White House and recalling the last of the occupying soldiers. Immediately thereafter the southern states removed blacks from office. Later they began in earnest to put the Negro "in his place."

◆᷿ JIM CROW

The Negro's "place" in society, although definitely inferior, was largely undefined by law for three decades after his emancipation. Throughout this period whites and blacks mingled unself-consciously, if superficially, in public places. And even when legal segregation or "Jim Crow" was first introduced, many white southerners ridiculed the idea. As one South Carolina editor mocked in 1898:

If there must be Jim Crow cars on the railroads, there should be Jim Crow cars on the street railways. Also on passenger boats . . . If there are to be Jim Crow cars, moreover, there should be Jim Crow sections of the jury box, and a separate Jim Crow dock and witness stand in every court—and a Jim Crow Bible for colored witnesses to kiss.

But what the editor looked upon as absurdity, an insecure white population made into reality—down to the Jim Crow

Bible. As Negroes exercised their right to vote, raised their literacy rate from 5 to 60 per cent and inched upward economically, they posed more of a threat to white supremacy than ever before. Poor whites who had to compete with them for jobs were particularly resentful of the blacks' progress. In order to artificially raise their own status, these poor whites—and many prosperous people, too—wanted the Negro to be made legally inferior, as he had been during slavery. They got their wish in 1896, when the Supreme Court condoned "separate but equal" accommodations for the races in the case of *Plessy v. Ferguson.*

Suddenly the South was gripped by a Jim Crow mania. Hotels, restaurants, hospitals, and cemeteries became segregated by law. Railroad cars, waiting rooms and rest rooms were designated "Colored" or "Whites Only." The passion for separation grew so strong that in South Carolina black and white cotton mill workers were not allowed to look out the same window and in Birmingham, Alabama, they could not play checkers in the same room! Needless to say, "separate" was almost never "equal." Where whites and Negroes did share the same facilities, discriminatory regulations kept the races apart. Some towns, for example, set aside auditoriums and fairgrounds for Negroes at certain times of the year and most southern cities allowed blacks to visit the public zoo one afternoon a week.

Although black people bitterly resented Jim Crow, they had neither the funds or the necessary white friends to fight it. Nor could they exert any political pressure because by 1910 nearly every black person in the South had been disfranchised. To accomplish this the southern states had instituted literacy and education tests for voters that few ex-slaves could pass. They demanded high poll taxes and other property requirements far above the limited means of sharecroppers. And where these "legal" methods failed they had used brute force. On several occasions Senator "Pitchfork" Ben Tillman of South Carolina boasted of the efforts to disfranchise Negroes in his state. "We have done our best," he said. "We have scratched our heads to find out how we could eliminate the last one of them. We stuffed ballot boxes. We shot them [Negroes]. We are not ashamed of it."

Between 1895 and 1915, while Jim Crow was spreading like a cancer into every facet of southern life, one man stood at the pinnacle of the Negro community. He dispensed more power than any black American before or since, and his first condemnation of segregation was published shortly after his death.

Booker T. Washington was born a slave. Emancipated at the age of nine, he got an education and went on to become a teacher. Then, while still a young man, he founded an agricultural and trade school named Tuskegee Institute. In 1895 Washington burst upon the national scene with a speech he made at the Cotton States Exposition in Atlanta, Georgia. In that address Washington urged Negroes to abandon their fight for social equality and to concentrate on improving their economic position through hard work instead. Holding up one hand, he declared dramatically, "In all things that are purely social we can be separate as the fingers, yet one as the hand in all things essential to mutual progress." After Washington finished, the whites in the audience leapt to their feet, cheering wildly. Yet, as one northern journalist noted, amidst the general glee "most of the Negroes in the audience were crying, perhaps without knowing why."

The so-called Atlanta Compromise made Booker T. Washington famous. White industrialists conferred with him before donating money to Negro causes and white politicians consulted him before appointing Negroes to political office. Steel magnate Andrew Carnegie gave Tuskegee $600,000 worth of United States Steel bonds, a good portion of them earmarked for Washington's personal use. President Theodore Roosevelt invited the black educator to dinner at the White House, a gesture that threw the South into an uproar. And among the masses of his own people, too, Washington was an acknowledged leader. His autobiography, *Up From Slavery,* was on the required reading list in hundreds of one-room Negro schools.

While Booker T. Washington was socializing with white businessmen and deciding on political appointments, caste lines hardened and lynchings increased in the South. Although he was not responsible for these developments, there is reason to believe his submissive attitude almost invited them. A few of Washington's contemporaries realized that he was having a harmful effect on the Negroes' struggle for equality and they spoke out against him. Leading the opposition was sociologist W.E.B. Du Bois. In his book, *The Souls of Black Folk,* Du Bois fired this broadside:

So far as Mr. Washington preaches Thrift, Patience, and Industrial Training for the masses, we must hold up his hands and strive with him. . . . But so far as Mr. Washington apologizes for injustices, North or South, does not rightly value the privilege and duty of vot-

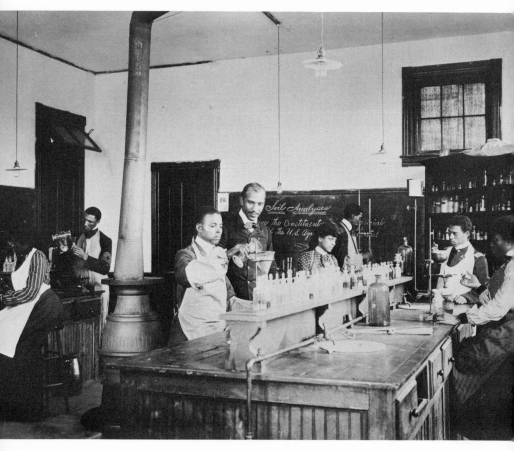

Convinced that Negroes would advance most rapidly if they knew farming or a trade, Booker T. Washington founded Tuskegee Institute to teach blacks practical skills. Here, a laboratory at Tuskegee. LIBRARY OF CONGRESS

ing, belittles the emasculating effects of caste distinctions, and opposes the higher training and ambition of our brighter minds—so far as he, the South or the Nation, does this—we must unceasingly and firmly oppose them.

In 1905 Du Bois brought together thirty prominent Negroes at Niagara Falls to map out a militant course of action for obtaining equal rights. The following year his group, which became known as the Niagara Movement, dramatized their cause by making a pilgrimage to Harper's Ferry. One morning at dawn they walked barefoot over the grass to the engine house where John Brown had made his last stand, and then, as the sun came up, they sang "The Battle Hymn of the Republic." On this occasion Du Bois issued one of his most stirring addresses, in which he declared:

We claim for ourselves every right that belongs to a free-born American—political, civil, and social—and until we get these rights, we will never cease to protest and assail the ears of America with the story of its shameful deeds toward us. We want full manhood suffrage, and we want it now, henceforth and forever.

Despite these fighting words the Niagara Movement accomplished very little. However, it did lay the groundwork for the influential National Association for the Advancement of Colored People. The N.A.A.C.P grew out of a race riot near Lincoln's grave in 1908, just a few months before the one hundredth anniversary of the Great Emancipator's birth. The riot's location and timing shocked into action a number of concerned whites. They approached the Niagara Movement about holding an interracial conference and out of that meeting came the "N double A." From the first the organization fought segregation through the courts. Among its early successes were the invalidation of residential segregation and the removal of certain voting restrictions in the South. The N.A.A.C.P. also mounted an impressive propaganda campaign spearheaded by W.E.B. Du Bois himself. As editor of the organization's publication, the *Crisis,* Du Bois continued to effectively "protest and assail the ears of America."

✐ GOING NORTH

At the turn of the century some 90 per cent of all black Americans still lived in the South. But in the next few years a number of adventurous Negroes crossed the Mason-Dixon line. They found the wages higher, the working conditions better, and the air freer up north, discoveries which they communicated to their kinsmen back home. These messages caused a great stir in the South, where many Negroes had almost given up hope of improving their situation. Lured by the promise of jobs, over one million Negroes trekked north between 1916 and 1923. The advance guard came from the border states of the old Confederacy, but after 1915, when swarms of boll weevils devoured the cotton crops, many blacks left the deep South as well.

Big business, which was then situated almost exclusively in the North, encouraged the migration because it needed cheap labor. The outbreak of World War I prevented the immigration of southern and eastern Europeans, American industry's major source of unskilled workers. Faced with a labor shortage just when the Allies were clamoring for its goods, big business broke with tradition and hired Negroes for the first time. Some companies even sent recruiters down South to entice black workers with railroad tickets and stories of golden opportunities with their firms. Migrants who settled in the Middle West generally went to work in automobile plants, steel mills, and packinghouses. Those who settled in the East took jobs in shipyards, light industry, and the service trades.

In all these fields the migrants started out doing the most menial tasks. Indeed, nothing in their background as agricultural workers had prepared them for anything else. But, given the opportunity, some blacks could have moved up to skilled or supervisory positions. That they did not do so was the result of prejudice and the refusal of organized labor to accept them as members. A few parent unions did allow Negroes to form affiliated locals, but even these black unionists were not promoted on a par with whites. Negroes consistently earned low wages as a result of discriminatory practices. Yet Samuel Gompers, president of the American Federation of Labor, felt justified in condemning the blacks as "cheap men."

When the migrants arrived in the great industrial centers of the North, they felt confused and overwhelmed. Almost none of them had encountered the hectic pace of city life before. As one migrant recalled, "I was completely lost. . . . I was afraid to sleep the first night—so much noise. I thought the cars would finally stop running so I could rest." A few of the newcomers who never could adjust to the city returned home. Most remained, but the struggle for survival in the new, harsh environment often exacted a heavy personal toll.

For Negroes, as for so many other newcomers, the worst

Members of the 372nd Colored Infantry, Boston,
Massachusetts, parading during World War I.
A few Armed Forces units remained segregated
until the Korean War broke out in 1950.
UNITED PRESS INTERNATIONAL PHOTO

feature of urban life was housing. The migrants quickly outgrew existing Negro enclaves, yet when they tried to move elsewhere they found that better neighborhoods were either closed to blacks or too expensive for them. Therefore, great numbers of poor, disorganized country people began to pile up in dilapidated buildings. Slums were born—and with them the alcoholism, dope addiction, prostitution, and crime which flourish under such unhappy circumstances. Every "new" immigrant group endured the hardships of slum living, often in the very same surroundings. But the Europeans were able to move out when they began to earn more money. And with more elbow room and less troubled neighbors, many of their problems disappeared. But few blacks could follow them out of the slums. Racial prejudice made Negroes prisoners of the city ghettos, where thirteen million of them now live.

As the ghettos took shape they began to develop many of the features of immigrant communities. Blacks opened restaurants, night clubs, barbershops, beauty parlors, funeral homes, and cosmetics businesses to cater to their own needs. They formed insurance companies, and savings and loan associations. And they started some voluntary organizations such as the Urban League, which aided migrants with their housing and employment problems. During the Great Migration northern ghettos also produced a crop of distinguished newspapers. These journals made a point of uncovering discrimination and boosting morale as well as reporting ethnic news. *The Chicago Defender, The Pittsburgh Courier, The New York Age,* and others gave blacks what one historian called their "weekly shot of racial adrenalin."

Every Negro newspaper devoted a great deal of space to religious activities because the Protestant church was at the center of ghetto life. In fact, it was the only institution in which the average black man participated. Religion had sustained southern Negroes since slave days and, when they migrated north, they brought their church-going habits with them. Even while the migrants were struggling to get established in their new homes, they contributed generously to church building funds. Soon ghettos across the nation boasted fine religious edifices, well-staffed and with a variety of related organizations and activities. These large churches usually belonged to the African Methodist Episcopal (A.M.E.), A.M.E. Zion and Baptist denominations. They drew parishioners who were middle-class in outlook if not in income. The small storefront churches, on the other hand, usually housed evangelical sects. They appealed to those members of the community who enjoyed the uninhibited fervor of revival meetings.

As blacks continued to leave Dixie, a serious "Negro problem" developed in the North. White workers did not like competing with the newcomers for jobs and white homeowners did not like having them as neighbors. In fact, should a black family try to integrate an all-white neighborhood, it was likely to have a bomb thrown into its living room. Racism grew particularly virulent in the North following World War I. The Ku Klux Klan, originally a southern terrorist organization, now flourished above the Mason-Dixon line as well as below it. Although racists made several assaults on "new" immigrants, they singled out Negroes for particular violence. But this time the blacks were prepared to fight back. During the "Red Summer" of 1919 twenty-six race riots flared across the nation. In Chicago blacks and whites met in pitched battle for thirteen days. The immediate cause of the encounter: a black boy swimming into a white beach area was met by a hail of stones and had drowned while trying to escape.

With discrimination, *de facto* segregation, and the threat of violence all around them, many migrants became disillusioned with the North. They grew pessimistic and cynical about their chances for a decent life in America. Correctly assaying their mood, Marcus Garvey promised to lead his fellow black men, spiritually at least, back to their true Promised Land— Africa. Upon that pledge Garvey built the first mass movement in Negro history. He appealed to the dispirited migrants with colorful parades, "African" courts, and chauvinistic speeches in which he glorified everything black. Speaking before his Universal Negro Improvement Association, the black Moses thundered, "Up, you mighty race, you can accomplish what you will!" Marcus Garvey's flamboyant showmanship netted the U.N.I.A. an estimated $10,000,000 in contributions, a fabulous sum for any Negro organization. He used this money to start a number of all-black businesses including a steamship line. But the Jamaican-born leader had no head for commerce and every one of his ventures collapsed. He was jailed in 1925 for using the mails with intent to defraud and he was deported two years later. Yet despite Garvey's inglorious end, black nationalism continued to exert a certain fascination for some Negroes.

Marcus Garvey reached the peak of his popularity in

1921. At about the same time so much high-caliber creativity began to pour forth from black ghettos, particularly from Harlem, that the 1920's became known as the "Negro Renaissance." During this era, moreover, black creativity was matched by a new white receptivity. White people bought paintings from black artists, read books by black authors, went to shows to watch black actors and flocked to nightclubs to listen to blues and jazz, the original "soul" music. Speaking of that heady era, Langston Hughes, one of the principal figures of the "Negro Renaissance" recalled: "It was a period when local and visiting royalty were not at all uncommon in Harlem. . . . It was a period when every season there was at least one hit play on Broadway acted by a Negro cast. . . . It was the period when the Negro was in vogue."

During the 1920's it was fashionable to speak of the "New Negro." Black youths were going on to high school, college, and even graduate school in increasing numbers. Negro professionals and businessmen were becoming so prosperous that owning an automobile was no longer a status symbol among them. And with flush times black workingmen, too, were beginning to see an improvement in their financial situation. During the 1920's, moreover, Negroes were becoming politically powerful in the North. In 1928 Oscar DePriest of Chicago became the first black man in thirty years to be elected to the House of Representatives. Adding up these achievements in early 1929, Negroes had reason to be optimistic about their future. But in September of that year the stock market crashed.

The Great Depression was nothing short of a disaster for

black America. The "last hired" in good times, blacks now found themselves "the first fired" when business retrenched after the crash. Negroes were even pushed out of their traditional menial jobs by whites who would have scorned such low-paying work in better times. By 1935, 25 per cent of all American Negroes were on relief and in northern cities that figure soared to 50 per cent and higher. Blacks became so desperate that they offered to work for ten cents an hour and some men even bartered their services for food. Whole Negro communities survived on the meager incomes of domestics. During the 1930's the Congress of Industrial Organizations unionized many Negroes when it organized automobile, steel, and other basic industries. But despite the C.I.O.'s efforts, the black community was still in dire economic straits as the decade drew to a close.

The Negro had made some political advances, though, after Franklin D. Roosevelt became President in 1933. Roosevelt invited many Negro leaders to the White House and he retained a "Black Cabinet" to advise him on racial affairs. Moreover, his relief programs, such as the Works Progress Administration, brought benefits to black as well as white Americans. Franklin Roosevelt gave Negroes a greater sense of "belonging" than ever before. Nevertheless, the President refused, for political reasons, to press for a Federal anti-lynching law and much New Deal legislation overlooked the poor black worker. It remained for World War II to bring vast new economic opportunities to Negroes and to provide the turning point in their struggle for equal rights.

♔ FREEDOM NOW

As it had during World War I, mobilization was opening new doors to Negroes on the eve of World War II. But this time blacks were not going to take second-best: they wanted completely integrated working conditions. A. Philip Randolph, president of the Brotherhood of Sleeping Car Porters, and other leaders threatened President Roosevelt with a mammoth "March on Washington" if this demand was not met. March on Washington committees held spirited rallies to raise money for the event and every segment of the Negro community enthusiastically endorsed it. Then, with the March scheduled to take place in just five days, President Roosevelt bowed to the pressure. He issued his famous Executive Order 8802 barring discrimination in defense industries and government because of "race, creed, color or national origin" and establishing the Fair Employment Practices Committee to investigate complaints of such discrimination.

By sheer necessity, business would have had to hire and upgrade Negro workers, but the F.E.P.C. greatly accelerated this process. Between 1941 and 1945 over a million blacks entered industry for the first time and the number of skilled and semi-skilled Negro workers doubled. Indeed, the black community witnessed more occupational diversification during the war than in the preceding seventy-five years. Moreover, although the F.E.P.C. was just a wartime measure, cities and states used it as a model for their own anti-discrimination laws and Congress patterned the equal employment opportunities section of the 1964 Civil Rights Act on it. The March on Washington—

America's inner cities are faced with an acute   [269] housing shortage. While old ghetto buildings are deteriorating rapidly, relatively little low-income housing is being built to replace them.
ROGERS, MONKMEYER

which was called off—also had important implications for the future. It solidified the Negro community and initiated mass participation in the civil rights movement. The idea behind the March, effecting change through peaceful but direct action, became the blacks' major strategy in the postwar era.

During World War II over one million Negroes served in the Armed Forces. Although they attained higher rank and greater concessions than in World War I, they still suffered the humiliation of discrimination and segregation. Never again, blacks vowed, would they fight a war to make the world safe for democracy—while they remained behind the lines in Jim Crow units. In 1948 A. Philip Randolph again took the lead, threatening a mass civil disobedience campaign against the draft if the Army was not desegregated. Now it was President Harry Truman who felt pressured and he, too, responded by issuing an executive order, this time calling for "equality of treatment and opportunity for all persons in the armed services. . . ."

The Korean War, which broke out two years later, provided the first opportunity to test integration on the battlefield. It worked so well that the last of the segregated units was abolished. Segregation and discrimination also disappeared from Army housing, training camps, and officers training schools. In fact, the military situation turned around so completely that today many black men feel they have a better chance to get ahead in the Armed Forces than in civilian life. Their re-enlistment rate is now almost triple that of whites and, while blacks account for only 11 per cent of the population, they have represented over 20 per cent of the front-line troops in Viet Nam.

The new, bold approach to ending discrimination in industry, government, and the Armed Forces was also adopted by the N.A.A.C.P for its legal battles against Jim Crow. After World War II, N.A.A.C.P. lawyers decided to launch a frontal attack on segregation based on the claim that separation itself constitutes discrimination. This strategy yielded a number of successes, culminating in the Supreme Court's landmark decision of 1954, *Brown v. Board of Education.* Reversing the judgment handed down fifty-eight years earlier in *Plessy v. Ferguson,* the Court declared unanimously "that in the field of public education the doctrine of 'separate but equal' has no place. Separate educational facilities are inherently unequal." One year later the Court ordered the states to desegregate their public schools with "all deliberate speed." In some places integration went forward in a peaceful, orderly fashion. In others, notably Little Rock, Arkansas, rioting broke out and armed troops had to be called in to escort black children to white schools. But few educational facilities, north or south, achieved a meaningful racial balance. White resistance has been partially responsible for this situation, but at least equally important is the physical difficulty of integrating schools that lie buried deep within all-white or all-black neighborhoods.

Although *Brown v. Board of Education* did not bring about the hoped-for educational revolution, it did destroy the legal basis of segregation. The next step, implementation, began a year later when a tired Negro seamstress refused to give up her seat to a white person on a Montgomery, Alabama, bus. She was arrested and fined ten dollars. Montgomery's Negroes then staged a one-day boycott of the bus system to protest the arrest. Under the leadership of a twenty-six-year-old minister,

Martin Luther King, Jr., that one-day strike turned into a thirteen-month crusade to desegregate the city's buses and resulted in a movement that swept the entire South. Dr. King was able to mobilize the resistance of Montgomery's black community because he added something vital to the civil rights movement: the Negro church. By wrapping protest in the songs and symbols of Christianity, the young minister gave the masses something they could identify with. Moreover, his nonviolent approach based on Mahatma Gandhi's passive-resistance campaigns in India appealed to Negroes because it achieved results without the loss of a single black life.

Montgomery and Martin Luther King, Jr., became symbols of the Negro's new self-respect. Inspired by Dr. King's militancy, four North Carolina students sat down at a "white" Woolworth's lunch counter in 1960 and refused to leave when they were not served. Their "sit-in" captured the imagination of young America. Soon more than fifty thousand black and white students were using similar techniques to desegregate other public facilities and end discrimination in hiring. Well-disciplined in nonviolent practice, the demonstrators submitted quietly when arrested and refused to fight back when attacked. And, inevitably, the attacks came. Some of the worst incidents occurred when "Freedom Riders" traveled across the South to test integration in transportation facilities. At several stops angry white mobs dragged the demonstrators from their seats, beating them severely, and even burning the buses they used. But mobs were not solely responsible for the violence. Newspapers and television stations carried pictures of white policemen clubbing black demonstrators, setting vicious dogs on children, and knocking over women with high-power water hoses. These shocking scenes elicited such a hue and cry that the Government at last took a firm stand to guarantee equality to all. In 1963 President Kennedy proposed the first sweeping Civil Rights Act in eighty-eight years.

The great era of nonviolent civil rights demonstrations reached its emotional climax on August 28, 1963, with the March on Washington for Jobs and Freedom. Two hundred and fifty thousand Americans, about sixty thousand of them white, marched to the Lincoln Memorial in Washington, D.C., where they commemorated the one hundredth anniversary of the Emancipation Proclamation. Every major civil rights leader was in attendance and every one of them spoke about the need to pass the Civil Rights Act and the need for "Freedom Now!" Finally, after three hours of speeches, Martin Luther King, Jr., got up to make his address. No one remembers the words of that prepared text, but the extemporaneous remarks that followed have become famous:

I have a dream that one day, on the red hills of Georgia, sons of former slaves and the sons of former slaveowners will be able to sit down together at the table of brotherhood.

I have a dream that one day even the state of Mississippi, a state sweltering with the heat of injustice, sweltering with the heat of oppression, will be transformed into an oasis of freedom and justice.

I have a dream that my little children will one day live in a nation where they will not be judged by the color of their skin but by the content of their character. . . .

Let freedom ring from every hill and molehill of Mississippi. From every mountainside, let freedom ring. And when we allow freedom to

The 1963 March on Washington, shown here, was the high point of the non-violent civil rights movement. In the years that followed, black protest grew more bitter and less peaceful.

WORLD WIDE PHOTOS

ring, when we let it ring from every village, from every hamlet, from every state and every city, we will be able to speed up that day when all of God's children, black men and white men, Jews and Gentiles, Protestants and Catholics, will be able to join hands and sing in the words of the old Negro spiritual: "Free at last! free at last! thank God Almighty, we are free at last!"

But the dream seemed destined to remain just that—a vision. Schools, neighborhoods, and labor unions remained segregated in fact, if not in law. And far from becoming more sympathetic to the Negro's cause, the rest of America either lost interest in civil rights or joined the ominous "white backlash." Ghetto-dwellers saw only menial labor, poverty, and slums for themselves while the TV flaunted good jobs, record prosperity, and split-level houses for the rest of America. True, the Government did enact the Civil Rights Act of 1964 and the Voting Rights Act of 1965. But at the same time it took funds from anti-poverty programs that would have aided many poor Negroes and spent them on the Viet Nam War. Finally, blacks grew tired of waiting for the dream to come true. After minor interracial incidents—often involving the police—great mobs took to the street burning, looting, and sniping. Their cries of "Burn, baby, burn!" increasingly drowned out the freedom song of nonviolent protestors, "We Shall Overcome." As ghetto after ghetto in Newark, Watts, Detroit, New York, and other cities went up in flames, Americans began to dread the long, hot summer.

Out of these chaotic conditions came "Black Power," a slogan which is used by different people to mean different things. When extremists call for "Black Power" they are usually

The late Dr. Martin Luther King, Jr., Floyd McKissick, Stokley Carmichael, Eldridge Cleaver, Julian Bond. These and other leaders have appealed to diverse segments of the Negro population. So far, however, no one has emerged as a spokesman for the entire black community. UNITED PRESS INTERNATIONAL PHOTO

advocating a kind of black nationalism or reverse racism in which the black man completely dissociates himself from white America. Some extremist groups, such as the Black Panthers, encourage the use of force to redress the Negro's grievances. But when moderate Negroes—and they are the vast majority —speak of "Black Power" they are referring to a shift in goals from immediate integration to the development of group strength. As part of their political coming of age, Negroes now want to control the anti-poverty programs, urban renewal projects, and schools in the communities in which they live. If European immigrants were arriving en masse in the United States today, no doubt they too would be organizing along these lines.

In addition to its political meaning, "Black Power" also indicates a new search for group identification and race pride. Negroes want to end for all time what W.E.B. Du Bois referred to as "this double-consciousness, this sense of always looking at one's self through the eyes of others." They have chosen their own labels, "black" or "Afro-American," and, under the banner "Black is Beautiful" they are determined to create their own standards of beauty. Denied a past by slavery, blacks are now trying to establish their own distinctive cultural heritage. They are demanding black studies programs in schools and universities so that they can familiarize themselves with Negro art, music, literature, and history in America and the rest of the world, particularly Africa. Even before the days of "Black Power," of course, Negroes identified with Africa and closely followed its anticolonial struggle. But the current interest in African clothing, dances, and culture indicates that blacks feel a new, more personal involvement with their ancestral homeland than ever before.

TO BRING FORTH A NEW NATION

America's treatment of the Negro has no parallel in immigration history. First through slavery and then through segregation the United States *legally* denied blacks the same right to "life, liberty and the pursuit of happiness" which it accorded Europeans as they stepped off the boat. Later, when Negroes began their Great Migration, whites made discrimination almost as formidable a barrier to advancement in the North as segregation had been in the South. Americans discriminated against Europeans, too, on cultural grounds—but cultural prejudice was never as thorough-going as racial prejudice. Moreover, the immigrants' children could escape by changing their names or moving out of the ghetto. But blacks, encased in the mark of their differentness, would remain highly visible in generation after generation. For all these reasons the Government had to take strong legal measures to help Negroes where it could officially ignore immigrants.

And so the great civil rights battles were waged and won and Jim Crow was buried for all time. Starting with World War II Negroes began to enjoy real equality of opportunity. Their new acceptance coupled with an unprecedented economic boom have enabled tens of thousands of blacks to move out of poverty each year, many of them achieving middle class economic status. One-third of the black population is now classified as "poor" compared to 56 per cent only ten years ago. Thanks to the civil rights movement, too, racial barriers have been falling in every facet of American life. Indeed, hardly a month goes by that another Negro "first" is not proclaimed. And through the exposure they have been getting in the mass media, blacks are no longer America's "invisible man." Ironically, this upward mobility is partially responsible for the increase in racial tension in recent years. For each time a Negro moves into a previously all-white domain, somebody inevitably feels threatened.

The advances of the last thirty years have been little short of miraculous. Yet today blacks still earn little more than half of what whites do and their unemployment rate runs twice as high. Nor are prospects bright for narrowing the gap. Opportunities are decreasing in agriculture and 40 per cent of the South's black population still lives on the farm. Automation is threatening to do away with manual labor and 80 per cent of the city's black workers hold blue collar jobs. As our society becomes more complex, it will be demanding better-educated workers. Already, most white collar jobs require a high school diploma or some college credits. Yet almost a quarter of all Negroes in their twenties have not gone beyond the eighth grade and 40 per cent have not completed high school.

If we are ever going to break the cycle of poverty and rebuild our cities, America must embark upon a massive rehabilitation program. Such a domestic Marshall Plan would be harder to implement than desegregation because it requires vast sums of money and an all-out national commitment. But America could do it. The country has the wealth and expertise and, as the space program proved, it also has a certain genius for rising to the challenge. The two hundredth anniversary of the birth of the Republic would make an excellent target date for such a project. As it is, blacks have had to wait too long to realize the American dream.

Suggested Reading

Bennett, Lerone, Jr. *Before the Mayflower: A History of the Negro in America, 1619–1964* (revised edition). Baltimore: Penguin Books, 1966.

Benson, Adolph B. and Naboth Hedin. *Americans from Sweden*. Philadelphia: J. B. Lippincott, 1950.

Berthoff, Rowland T. *British Immigrants in Industrial America, 1790–1950*. Cambridge: Harvard University Press, 1953. Includes all the British Isles.

Franklin, John Hope and Isidore Starr. (editors). *The Negro in Twentieth Century America*. New York: Random House, 1967.

Glazer, Nathan and Daniel P. Moynihan. *Beyond the Melting Pot: the Negroes, Puerto Ricans, Jews, Italians and Irish of New York City*. Cambridge: M.I.T. Press, 1963.

Handlin, Oscar. *Boston's Immigrants, 1790–1865*. Cambridge: Harvard University Press, 1941.

———. *Immigration as a Factor in American History*. Englewood Cliffs: Prentice-Hall, 1959. Source material.

———. *The Newcomers: Negroes and Puerto Ricans in a Changing Metropolis*. Cambridge: Harvard University Press, 1959.

Hansen, Marcus Lee. *The Atlantic Migration 1607–1860*. Cambridge: Harvard University Press, 1940.

—————. *The Immigrant in American History*. Cambridge: Harvard University Press, 1940. Essays.

Hapgood, Hutchins. *The Spirit of the Ghetto*. New York: Funk and Wagnalls, 1909.

Higham, John. *Strangers in the Land: Patterns of American Nativism 1860–1925*. New York: Atheneum, 1963.

Italians of New York, The. Prepared by workers of the Federal Writers Project, W.P.A. New York: Random House, 1938.

Lee, Rose Hum. *The Chinese in the United States of America*. Hong Kong: Hong Kong University Press, 1960.

Lengyel, Emil. *Americans from Hungary*. Philadelphia: J. B. Lippincott, 1948.

Malcolm X. *The Autobiography of Malcolm X*. New York: Grove Press, 1964. Black nationalism and the Negro experience.

O'Connor, Richard. *The German-Americans*. Boston: Little, Brown, 1968.

Riis, Jacob A. *How the Other Half Lives*. London: Sampson Low, Marston, Searle and Rivington, 1891.

Rölvaag, O. E. *Giants in the Earth*. New York: Harper and Row, 1927. Novel about Norwegian pioneers.

Saloutos, Theodore. *The Greeks in the United States*. Cambridge: Harvard University Press, 1963.

Sexton, Patricia Cayo. *Spanish Harlem*. New York: Harper and Row, 1965.

Shannon, William V. *The American Irish*. New York: Macmillan, 1963.

Smith, Abbot Emerson. *Colonists in Bondage: White Servitude and Convict Labor in America 1607–1776*. Chapel Hill: University of North Carolina Press, 1947.

Smith, Bradford. *Americans from Japan*. Philadelphia: J. B. Lippincott, 1948.

Solomon, Barbara Miller. *Ancestors and Immigrants*. Cambridge: Harvard University Press, 1956. Study of New England nativism.

Index